27th Consecutive Issu

FOUNDED 193

By Victor H. Green

K

1963-64 EDITION

Published by
VICTOR H. GREEN CO.

L. A. WALLER
MELVIN TAPLEY
Co-Publishers

This edition of Travelers' Green Book is dedicated to our many friends and advertisers whose cooperation and encouragement made it possible: Mrs. Alma Green, Reginald Pierrepointe, Carlton Bertrand, Atty. J. J. Fieulleteau, Atty. Hope Stevens, Constance Curtis, Al Lockhart, William Capitman, Hy Schneider, Wendell Colton, Peter Celliers, Ken Brown, Thomasina Norford, Dr. P. M. H. Savory, Ted Shearer, Vondel Nichols, Frank Palumbo, and YOU.

INSIDE

Features:

LOCKHART AGENCY

Offices are located at 200 W. 135th St., New York 30, N. Y.

Cover by
WILLARD SMITH

RIGHTS GUARDIANS—Congressmen William L. Dawson, Ill.; Augustus C. Hawkins, Calif.; Adam C. Powell, N. Y.; Robert N. C. Nix, Pa.; Charles C. Diggs, Mich., are five stalwarts
ROBT. COTTROL

YOUR RIGHTS, BRIEFLY SPEAKING!

Most people who 'go on holiday,' as they say in England, the Caribbean and other places where the accent is English, are seeking someplace that offers them rest, relaxation and a refuge from the cares and worries of the work-a-day world.

The Negro traveler, to whom the Travelers Green Book has dedicated its efforts since 1936, is no exception. He too, is looking for "Vacation Without Aggravation".

Of course, this is no surprise. The National Association for the Advancement of Colored People, the National Urban League, the Congress on Racial Equality, the Students Non-Violence Committee, the Southern Christian Leadership Association and other groups fighting for minority rights make it very clear that the Negro is only demanding what everyone else wants . . . what is guaranteed all citizens by the Constitution of the United States.

In fact, the militancy of these civil right groups exhibited in sit-ins, kneel-ins, freedom rides, other demonstration and court battles has widened the areas of public accommodations accessible to all.

Realizing that a family planning a vacation hopes for one that is free of tensions and problems, the Travelers Green Book includes the following brief summary of various state statutes on discrimination as they apply to public accommodations or recreation:

ALASKA Law bans jimcro in recreational facilities. Violators are subject to criminal punishment (court proceedings).

CALIFORNIA Anti-jimcro law in recreational facilities. Violators are subject to civil suits for damages plus $250.

COLORADO
CONNECTICUT Anti-jimcro law in recreational facilities, including discriminatory advertising. Administrative enforcement machinery. Alternatively, enforcement through court proceedings (criminal punishment).

DISTRICT OF COLUMBIA Anti-jimcro law in recreational facilities. Violators subject to criminal punishment, forfeiture of licenses (court proceedngs).

IDAHO Anti-jimcro in recreational facilities. Violators subject to criminal punishment (court proceedings).

ILLINOIS Anti-jimcro law in recreational facilities, including discriminatory advertising. Violators subject to civil damages, criminal punishment and injunction (court proceedings).

INDIANA	Anti-jimcro law in recreational facilities. Violators are subject to civil damages and criminal punishment (court proceedings).
IOWA	. . . Violators subject to criminal punishment (court proceedings).
KANSAS	. . . Violators subject to fines (court proceedings).
MAINE	. . . including discriminatory advertising. Violators subject to criminal punishment (court proceedings).
MASSACHUSETTS	. . . including . . . advertising. Administrative enforcement machinery. Alternatively, enforcement through court proceedings (civil damages, criminal punishment).
MICHIGAN	. . . including . . . advertising. Violators are subject to civil suits for treble damages, criminal punishment, and revocation or suspension of license (court proceedings).
MINNESOTA	. . . Violators subject to civil damages and criminal punishment . . .
MONTANA	. . . No specific sanctions.
NEBRASKA	. . . Violators subject to criminal punishment (court proceedings).
NEVADA	Law declares jimcro in recreational facilities to be against public policy. Administrative investigating machinery.
NEW HEMPSHIRE	. . . Violators subject to fines . . .
NEW JERSEY	. . . including discriminatory advertising. Administrative enforcement machinery. Alternatively, enforcement through court proceedings (civil damages, criminal punishment).
NEW MEXICO	. . . No specific sanctions.
NEW YORK OREGON PENNSYLVANIA	. . . including discriminatory advertising. Administrative enforcement machinery. Alternatively, enforcement through court proceedings (civil damages, criminal punishment).
NORTH DAKOTA	. . . Violators subject to criminal punishment . . .
OHIO	. . . Administrative enforcement machinery. Alternatively, enforcement through court proceedings (civil damages, criminal punishment).
RHODE ISLAND	. . . Administrative enforcement machinery.
VERMONT	. . . Violators subject to criminal punishment (court proceedings).
VIRGINIA	Prohibition of advertisements discriminating because of religion. Violators are liable to injunction suits (court proceedings).
VIRGIN ISLANDS	. . . Violators subject to civil damage (actual damages plus punitive damages up to $5000), criminal punishment and revocation or suspension of licenses (court proceedings).
WASHINGTON	. . . including discriminatory advertising. Administrative enforcement machinery. Alternatively, enforcement through court proceedings . . .
WEST VIRGINIA	No law prohibiting discrimination in recreational facilities. Human Rights Commission authorized to investigate charges of discrimination.
WISCONSIN	. . . . Violators subject to civil damages and criminal punishment. . .
WYOMING	. . . Violators subject to criminal punishment . . .

This information was condensed from "Civil Rights and Minorities" by Paul Hartman, associate director of the law department of the Anti-Defamation League of B'nai B'rith. Other excellent reference material is the "Report On State Anti-Discrimination Agencies and the Laws They Administer" prepared by the Commission on Law and Social Action of the American Jewish Congress. Shad Polier is chairman of the Commission; Leo Pfeffer, director; and Joseph Robison, assistant director. Mr. Robison is author of these AJC reports.

By-the-way, if you encounter any problems in these states that have this legislation (incidentally, Massachusetts had a law banning discrimination in recreational facilities open to the general public as far back as 1865 . . . the first of its kind) you can take your complaint to:

Alaska — Dept. of Labor — Juneau, Alaska

California — Div. of Fair Employment Practices, Dept. of Industrial Relations — 455 Golden Gate Ave., San Francisco 1, Calif.

Colorado — Anti-Discrimination Commission — 1525 Sherman St., Denver

Connecticut — Commission on Civil Rights — State Office Bldg., Hartford 15

Illinois — Fair Employment Practices Commission — Chicago

Indiana — Civil Rights Commission — 1004 State Office Bld., Indianapolis 4, Ind.

Kansas — Commission on Civil Rights — State Office Bldg., Topeka, Kan.

Massachusetts — Commission Against Discrimination—41 Tremont St., Boston, Mass.

Michigan — Fair Employment Practice Commission — 900 Cadillac Sq. Bldg., Detroit 26, Mich.

Minnesota — Minnesota Fair Employment Practices Commission — Rm. 12, State Office Bldg., St. Paul 1

Missouri — Commission on Human Rights — Rm 131B, State Capitol Bldg., Jefferson City, Mo.

New Jersey — Div. on Civil Rights, Dept. of Education — 1100 Raymond Blvd., Newark 5, N. J.

New Mexico — Fair Employment Practices Commission — Capitol Bldg., Santa Fe, New Mexico

New York — Commission on Human Rights — 270 Broadway, N. Y. 7

Ohio, Civil Rights Commission — 22 E. Gay St., Columbus 15

Oregon — Civil Rights Division, Bureau of Labor — 1216 S.W. Hall St., Portland 1

Pennsylvania — Human Relations Commission, Dept. of Labor and Industry — 1401 Labor & Industry Bldg., Harrisburg

Rhode Island — Commission Against Discrimination — State House, Providence 2

Washington — State Board Against Discrimination — 206 Capitol Park Bldfi., Olympia

Wisconsin — Fair Employment Practices Division — 634 2nd St., Milwaukee Industrial Commission

ALABAMA

Hotels — Motels — Tourist Homes — Restaurants

ATMORE

Paris Motel .... 173 Ashley Street

★The SNACK BAR .... 70 Carver Avenue
Where They Have A Knack For Delicious Snacks

★PALM LEAF HOTEL .... 328½ North 18th Street
Your Gracious Hostess . . . Mrs. Eva Lou Russell

★PARKVIEW CAFE & RAYMOND'S SNACK BAR .... 1701 Fifth No.

DOTHAN

William Washington Hotel .... 216 W. North Street

FLORENCE

Hawkin's Bar-B-Que .... 837 W. Mobile Avenue

GADSDEN

Mrs. A. J. Shepard Tourist Home .... 1324 4th Avenue
Barnes Motel .... 422 North 9th Street
James Service Station & Body Shop .... 213 N. 6th Street

James Sundry & Snack Bar .... 554 Meighan Blvd.

Skyline Recreation Center .... 550-C Meighan Blvd.
The Marisue Apartment & Motel .... 550-C Meighan Blvd.

HUNTSVILLE

Glaly's Jane Motel .... 1302 Posey Avenue
Mrs. India Herndon Tourist Home .... 515 Oak Street
Mrs. Rose Allen Tourist Home .... 212 Lowe Street
Patten Service Station .... 329 North Church Street

MOBILE

E. Jordan Tourist Home .... 256 North Dearborn Street
F. Wildins Tourist Home .... 254 North Dearborn Street
Le Grand Hotel .... 1461 Davis Avenue

MONTGOMERY

Alexander's Blue & Gray Inn .... 1415 Wilcox
Hotel Ben Moore .... 902 Highland Avenue
Mrs. Dave Sims Tourist Home .... 900 Cleveland Avenue
Mrs. Dave Sims Tourist Home .... 322 Cleveland Street

MOULTON

Triangle Shopping Center .... Sommerville Avenue

PHENIX CITY

Rayfus Parham Tire Shop & Service Station .... 1725 Seale Road

TUSCALOOSA

G. W. Clopton Tourist Home .... 1516 25th Avenue
Hotel Preston .... 101 University Avenue

TUSKEGEE

Flossie's Fashion .... Carver Shopping Center, Southside & Jericho Streets
Gunn's Grocery, Garage & Gas .... 2 Mi. East of Tuskegee

TUSKEGEE INSTITUTE

Rogers Shoe Shop & Shoe Store, Inc. .... Phone 944
Snowden's Garage & OK Rubber Welders .... Phone 582
Typewriter Sales & Service Co. .... Chambliss Bldg.
Wiley's Eat Shop .... Montgomery Hiway, U.S. 80 at Greenforks

ALASKA

Hotels — Motels — Tourist Homes — Restaurants

ANCHORAGE

Parsons Hotel .... 300 M Street
The Westward Hotel .... 3rd Ave. & F St.
Traveler's Inn .... 720 Gambell Street

FAIRBANKS

Fairbanks Hotel
Savoy Hotel
Traveler's Inn .... 813 Noble Street

JUNEAU

Baranof Hotel .... 2nd & Franklin St.

KETCHIKAN

The Ingersoll Hotel .... Front & Mission St.

ARIZONA

Hotels — Motels — Tourist Homes — Restaurants

BISBEE

Hotel Copper Queen

DOUGLAS

Faustina Wilson Tourist Home .... 1002 16th Street

FLAG STAFF

El Rancho Flag Staff .... Box 1241
Park Plaza Motel .... Rts. 66 & 89

GRAND CANYON

Bright Angle
El Toya Hotel

KINGMAN

Mountain Villa Motel .... Hwy. 66, East
★**White Rock Court** .... **843 E. Andy Dr.**

MESA

Peter Pan Motel .... 620 Main St.

NOGALES

Coronado .... 900 Grand Ave.
El Porto Motel .... Tucon Road

PHOENIX

Alhambia Restaurant .... 1246-48 East Washington St.
Hotel Rice .... 535 East Jefferson Street
Lucille's Motel .... 2021 E. Van Buren St.
★PADUCAH HOTEL AND APARTMENTS .... **14 North 6th Street**
254-0938 — Reasonable Rates — Write for Reservations
Rose Restaurant .... 947 West Watkins Street
★SWINDALL'S TOURIST HOME .... **1021 East Washington St.**

PRESCOTT

Mission Lodge .... 1211 E. Gurley

TUCSON

Mrs. Louise Pitts Tourist Home .... 722 North Perry Street
Rio Motel .... 3031 So. 6th

YUMA

Rev. James Coleman's Downtown Lodge
113 S. Gila Street
Yuma, Arizona

ARKANSAS

Hotels — Motels — Tourist Homes — Restaurants

ARKADELPHIA

Hill's Hotel .... 1601 West Pine Street

BLYTHESVILLE

St. Francis Sundry Store .... 1204 Heans Street

CAMDEN

Burnell's Service Station .... 204 Grinstead S. E.
Mrs. Benjamin Williams .... North Main Street

CONWAY

Deluxe Diner .... 1151 Markham Street

ELDORADO

C. W. Moore Tourist Home .... 618 Cordell
Dr. Dunning Tourist Home .... 709 Columbia Avenue
Green's Hotel .... 303 Hill Street

FAYETTEVILLE

N. Smith Tourist Home .... 259 East Center Street

FORDYSE

Harlem Restaurant .... 211 1st Street

FORT SMITH

Mrs. Clara Oliver Tourist Home .... 718 North 9th Street
Ullery Inn Hotel .... 719 North 9th Street

HELENA

Barbour's Tourist Home .... 814 Richtor St.

HOPE

Green Leaf Restaurant .... Highway 67
Lewis-Wilson Hotel .... 217 East 3rd Street

HOT SPRINGS

Arkansas Loan Company .... 428 Malvern Avenue
Barabin Villa .... 717 Pleasant Street
C. & D. Hotel .... 320 Church Street
Crittenden Hotel .... 314 Cottage Street
Gray's Hotel .... 436 Church Street
Harris Hotel .... Church & Cottage Sts.
Home Rooms for Rent .... $10.50—$6.50 week .... 120 Gaines Ave.
J. W. Rife Tourist Home .... 347½ Malvern Avenue
Jewell Apartments .... 711 Pleasant Street
Little Palace Cafe .... 403½ Silver Street
★McKENZIE MOTEL .... 401 Henry St., 2 blocks off Hwy. 270 East
South's Finest — Air Conditioned — Phone NA 3-7849
National Baptist Sanitarium .... 501 Malvern Ave.
New Edmondson Tourist Home .... 207 Ash Street
Palm Lounge Restaurant .... 415 Malvern Ave.
Pythian Baths .... 415½ Malvern St.
Rest-A-While Tourist Home .... 121 Grove St.

Smith's Steak House .... 435 Malvern Avenue
The Harlem Chicken Shack .... 518 Malvern Avenue
The Royal Liquor Store .... 526 Malvern Avenue
The Texan Inn .... 605 Pleasant Street
Town Talk Barbeque .... 500 Pleasant St.
Wadkins Tourist Home .... 212 Garden St.

LITTLE ROCK

College Restaurant .... 16th and Bishop
Graysonia Hotel .... 809 Gaines Street
Honeycut Hotel .... 816 West 9th Street
Miller Hotel .... 812½ West 9th Street
Mrs. H. Gilmore Tourist Home .... 1324 West 19th St.
Tucker's Hotel .... 701½ West 9th Street

MADISON

U. S. Bond's Motel .... U. S. Hway. 70, ½ mile w. of Madison

NORTH LITTLE ROCK

Cat's Motel & Cafe .... Highway 67W
De Lux Court .... 2720 East Broadway
Ideal Beauty Shop .... Rt. 5, Box 360
Jim's Restaurant .... 908 Cedar Street N.L.R.
Nov-Vena Restaurant .... 1101 East 6th Street
Waters Drive-In .... Rt. 5, Box 360

PINE BLUFF

Duck Inn Restaurant .... 405 North Cedar Street
M. J. Hollis Tourist Home .... 1108 West 2nd Avenue
Pee Kay Hotel .... 300 East 3rd Street

RUSSELLVILLE

E. Latimore Tourist Home .... 318 South Huston Avenue

TEXARKANA

Brown's Hotel .... 312 West Elm Street
G. C. Mackey Tourist Home .... 102 East 9th Street
Grant's Cafe Restaurant .... 830 Laurel Street

TUCKERMAN

Freeman's Tourist Court .... Hwy. 67

WEST MEMPHIS

CALIFORNIA

Hotels — Motels — Tourist Homes — Restaurants

ALTURAS

Niles .... P. O. Box 891

ANAHEIM

Disneyland .... 1441 So. West Street

BERKELEY

Berkeley Inn .... 2501 Taste St.
Berkeley Plaza .... 1175 University Ave.
Bonanza Motel .... 1720 San Pablo Ave.
Claremont Hotel .... Ashby and Claremont Ave.
Durant Hotel .... 2600 Durant Ave.

FRESNO

De Lux Restaurant .... 2193 Ivy Street
Fresno Hacienda .... Hwy. 99 and Clinton
Palm Motel .... Hwy. 99, North
Poplar Grove Motel .... Hwy. 99

HOLLYWOOD

Carlton Lodge .... 2011 N. Highland Ave.
Hollywood Plaza .... 1637 N. Vine
Hollywood Roosevelt .... 7000 Hollywood Blvd.
Hallmark House Motor Hotel .... 7023 Sunset Blvd.
Hollywood Thunderbird Inn .... 8300 Sunset Blvd.
Hollywood Wilcox Hotel .... 6500 Selma Ave.
Imperial "400" Motel .... 6826 W. Sunset Blvd.
Sands-Sunset Hotel .... 8775 Sunset Blvd.

LOS ANGELES

Alexandria .... 210 W. 5th Street
Ambassador .... 3400 Wilshire Blvd.
Astor Motel .... 2901 S. Flower St.
Bel Air Motel .... 701 Stone Canyon Rd.
Biltmore .... 515 S. Olive Street
Californian .... 1907 W. 6th Street
★CASBAH APARTMENTS AND ROOMS .... **1189 W. 36th Place**
Reasonable Rates — Comfort — Privacy — Good Accommodations
For Information and Reservations Write or Tel.: 735-8290
Clark .... 425 S. Hill Street
Cortez .... 375 Columbia Ave.
EC Eastsider .... 2133 S. Central
EC Motel .... 3501 S. Wesetrn
HAYES MOTEL .... **960 Jefferson Blvd.**
HAYES WESTERN MOTEL .... **3700 S. Western Avenue**
Harmon Motel .... 700 W. Florence
Manchester Motel .... 800 E. Manchester
Mayfair .... 1256 W. 7th Street
New Casa Motel .... 7720 S. Main St.
Notel Motel .... 4766 S. Main St.
PALM VUE .... **3922 South Western**
Raywood Motel .... 8200 S. Figueroa St.

Santa Barbara Motel .... 1758 W. Santa Barbara Ave.
Sky Terrace Motel .... Normandie & Jefferson Blvd.
Statler-Hilton .... 930 Wilshire Blvd.

LAKE ELSIMORE

Lake Elsimore Hotel .... 416 North Kelogg Street

MADERA

Casa Grand Motel .... Hwy. 99

NEEDLES

El Adobe Motel .... U. S. Highway 66

OAKLAND

California Hotel .... 3501 San Pablo Street
Carver Hotel .... 1412 Market Street
Fifty-Fifth Motel .... 2320 55th Ave.

PERRIS

Muse-A-While .... Highway 395

SACRAMENTO

Dunlop's Restaurant .... 4322 4th Ave.

SAN DIEGO

Douglas Hotel .... 206 Market St.
Ebony Inn Motel .... 740 32nd St.
Manor Hotel .... 2223 El Cajon Blvd.
Motel Western Shores .... 6345 Pacific Hwy.
Simmons Hotel .... 542 6th Avenue
Y.W.C.A. .... 1012 C. Street

SAN FRANCISCO

Booker T. Washington Hotel .... 1540 Ellis St.
Bullford Hotel .... 843 Hayes Street
Edison Hotel .... 1540 Ellis Street
New Pullman Hotel .... 232 Townsend Street
Sir Francis Drake Hotel .... 450 Powell St.
Texas Hotel .... 1840 Filmore Street
The Scaggs Hotel .... 1715 Webster Street

SAN LUIS OBISPO

Ranchotel .... 1900 Montgomery St.

STOCKTON

El Camino Motel .... 1506 Mariposa
Sunset Motel .... 1305 So. Wilson Way

VALLEJO

Bell Motel .... 1308 Lincoln Hwy.
Charlotte Hotel .... 518 Sacramento St.

YOSEMITE NATIONAL PARK

Camp Curry
Glasier Point Hotel
High Sierra Hotel
Hotel Ahwanne
Yosemite Lodge

COLORADO

Hotels — Motels — Tourist Homes — Restaurants

ADAMS CITY

Crestline Motor Hotel .... 7330 Hiway 85

COLORADO SPRINGS

G. Roberts Tourist Home .... 418 East Cucharras Street

GREELEY

Mrs. E. Alexander Tourist Home .... 106 East 12th St.

LA MAR

Alamo Hotel .... La Mar, Colorado

MESA VERDE NATIONAL PARK

Spruce Tree Lodge

MONTROSE

Adams Hotel .... Montrose, Colorado
Chipeta Cafe .... Montrose, Colorado

PUEBLO

Coronado Lodge .... 2130 Lake

CONNECTICUT

Hotels — Motels — Tourist Homes — Restaurants

BRIDGEPORT

Hotel Barnum .... 150 Fairfield
Arcade Hotel .... 1001 Main Street
Bridgeport Motor Inn .... 100 Kings Highway Cut-off
Rte 1A, Exit 24, Conn Turnpike
Stratfield Hotel .... 1241 Main Street

CLINTON

Clinton Hotel .... 14 E. Main Street
Coastway Motel .... U.S. Hwy No. 1

DANBURY

New Englander Motor Hotel .... Main Street

DARIEN

Howard Johnson's Motor Lodge .... Conn. Turnpike Exit 11

EAST HARTFORD

Howard Johnson's Motor Lodge .... 490 Main Street

GREENWICH

Indian Harbor Motel .... 34 E. Putnam Ave.
New Englander Motor Hotel .... 1114 Post Rd. (U.S. 1)

HARTFORD

Bond Hotel .... 338 Asylum St.
Farmington Ave. Motor Lodge .... 226 Farmington Ave.
Georgian Motor Hotel & Apts. .... 725 Asylum Ave.
Hartford Hotel .... 240 Church St.
Mrs. Johnson Tourist Home .... 2016 Main St.
Statler Hilton .... Ford and Pearl Streets

MOODUS

Banner Lodge .... Banner Rd.
Dawn Lodge .... TRiangle 3-9015
Moodie's Lodge .... TW 8-9573
Ted Hilton's .... Rte 151

NEW HAVEN

Duncan Hotel .... 1151 Chapel St.
Hotel Garde .... 4 Columbus Ave.
Howard Johnson's Motor Lodge .... 2260 Whitney Ave.
Monterey Restaurant .... 267 Dixwell Avenue
Nathan Hale Motor Inn .... 1605 Whalley Ave.

Rip Van Winkle Hotel .... 1548 Whalley Ave.
Taft Hotel .... Chapel & College St.
Three Judges Motel .... 1560 Whalley Ave.

NEW LONDON

Crocker House .... 178 State St.
Lighthouse Inn .... Lower Blvd.
Mohican Hotel .... 281 State St.
Mrs. E. Whittle Tourist Home .... 46 Hempstead St.

POMFRET CENTER

Willow Inn .... Highway 44, 1/2 Mile W. of Conn. Rts 101 & 44

SHARON

Gordon's Tourist Home

SOUTH NORWALK

Palm Gardens Hotel .... Post Road

STAMFORD

Robert Graham Tourist Home .... 37 Hanrahan Ave.

WATERBURY

Community House Tourist Home .... 34 Hopkins St.
Elton Hotel .... Waterbury, Conn.
Putt Meadow Motel .... U. S. Hwy. 6-A

WEST HAVEN

Dadds Hotel .... 359 Beach Street
Seaview Hotel .... 392 Beach Street
Dixon's .... 379 Beach Street
Home of Hawkins .... 372 Beach Street

DELAWARE

Hotels — Motels — Tourist Homes — Restaurants

DOVER

Dean's Hotel .... Forrest Street
Mosely's Hotel .... Division Street

LAUREL

Joe Randolph's Restaurant .... West 6th Street

REBOBOTH BEACH

Mallory Cabins .... Reboboth Avenue Ext.

TOWNSEND

Rodney Hotel .... Dupont Highway—Rt. 13

WILMINGTON

Christian Assn. Bldg. Restaurant .... 10th and Walnut St.
Miss W. A. Brown Tourist Home .... 1306 Tatnall Street
Y.M.C.A. .... 10th and Walnut Street

DISTRICT OF COLUMBIA

Hotels — Motels — Tourist Homes — Restaurants

WASHINGTON, D. C.

- **★ALFRED'S RESTAURANT .... 1610 "U" Street, N.W.**
- Ambassador Hotel .... Fourteenth & K Street, N.W.
- Bellevue Hotel .... 15 E. St., N.W.
- Buddie's Tourist Home .... 1320 5th Street
- Burlington Hotel .... 1120 Vermont Ave., N.W.
- Cadillac Hotel .... 1500 Vermont Street, N.W.
- Carlyle Hotel .... 500 N. Capital Street
- Commodore .... No. Capitol & F Street, N.W.
- Charles Hotel .... 1338 R Street, N.W.
- Clore Hotel .... 614 S Street, N.W.
- Cozy Restaurant .... 708 Florida Avenue, N.W.
- Dupont Plaza .... 1500 New Hampshire Avenue, N.W.
- Earl's Restaurant .... 1218 U Street, N.W.
- Edward's Tourist Home .... 1837 16th Street, N.W.
- Executive House .... Scott Circle, N.W.
- International Inn .... Thomas Circle, 14th & M Streets, N.W.
- Johnson, Jr. Hotel .... 1509 Vermont Avenue, N.W.
- Ken Rod Hotel .... 621 Rhode Island Ave., N.W.
- Kenyon Grill Restaurant .... 3119 Georgia Avenue, N.W.
- Madison .... 15th & M St., N.W.
- Manger Annapolis Hotel .... 1111 H Street, N.W.
- Manger Hamilton Hotel .... 14th & K St., N.W.
- Manger Hay-Adams Hotel .... 16th & H St., N.W.
- Modern Tourist Home .... 3006 13th St., N.W.
- Patsy's Tourist Home .... 2026 13th St., N.W.
- Pitts' Tourist Home .... 1451 Belmont St., N.W.
- Raleigh Hotel .... 12th St. & Pennsylvania Ave.
- Republic Gardens Restaurant .... 1355 U St., N.W.
- Rivers Tourist Home .... 1021 Monroe St., N.W.

Roger Smith Hotel .... Pennsylvania Ave. & 18th St., N.W.
Sheraton-Carlton Hotel .... 923 16th St., N.W.
Sheraton-Park Hotel .... Conn. Ave. & Woodley Rd., N.W.
Statler Hilton .... 16th & K Sts., N.W.
Sugar Bowl Restaurant .... 2830 Georgia Ave., N.W.
The Hour Restaurant .... 1837 11th St., N.W.
Towles Tourist Home .... 1321 13th St., N.W.
Y.M.C.A. .... 1816 12th St., N.W.
Y.M.C.A. .... 901 Rhode Island Ave., N.W.

FLORIDA

Hotels — Motels — Tourist Homes — Restaurants

COCONUT GROVE

Brown's Grove 66 Station .... 3685 Grand Avenue

BOYNTON BEACH

Bahama Motel .... 114½ N.E. 10th Ave.

DAYTONA

KAT TAVERN .... 325 Mississippi Street
Friendly Atmosphere .... Phone CL 2-9632

GRAY'S SERVICE STATION
Riley M. Gray, Prop.
693 Cypress St., Daytona Beach

Paradise Inn .... 328 Alabama Street
James Cooper, Mgr. .... Daytona Beach, Fla.

DELAND

DELRAY BEACH

Fifth Avenue Pharmacy .... 104 N. W. 5th Avenue
Kemp's Paradise Restaurant .... 103 N. W. 5th Avenue
La France Hotel .... 104 N. W. 5th Avenue

FERNANDINA BEACH

American Beach Apts.

FT. LAUDERDALE

Cooper's Sundries & Cafe .... 615 N. W. 6th Street
Catherine's Better Food Cafe .... 515 N. W. 4th Street
The Friendly Place to Find the Best Home Cooking
Chester's Place .... 1312 N. W. 5th Street
Osborn's Restaurant .... 1904 N. W. 6th Street
Five Point Service Station .... 2590 N. W. 22nd Rd.
Hankerson's Gulf Service Station .... 1201 N. W. 6th Street
Hill Hotel .... 430 N. W. 7th Avenue
Johnson's Service Station .... 1100 N. W. 6th Street
O'Dell's Bar & Grill & Rooms .... 2930 N. W. 7th Street
Tasty Luncheonette .... 315A N. W. 5th Avenue

HOLLYWOOD

Dew Drop Inn .... 2243 Simms Street

HOMESTEAD

Ida's Cafe .... 739 S. W. 8th Avenue

JACKSONVILLE

★ASTOR MOTEL .... 1111 Cleveland St., on U.S. #1 North
Jaxonville's FINEST STOP TO MIAMI Rates $5 up
Pvt. BATHS — AIR COND. — Leave U.S. 95 EXIT AT KINGS RD.

THE FIESTA MOTEL

One of the South's Finest In The Gateway City

Free TV • Private Bath with
Shower in Every Room.
Electrically Heated

1251 Kings Rd. Jacksonville, Fla.

B. Robinson Tourist Home .... 128 Orange Street
Blue Chip Hotel .... 514 Broad Street
C. H. Simmons Tourist Home .... 434 W. Ashley Street
Gwendolyn Hotel .... 722 W. Monroe Street

KEY WEST

Little Charles Hotel .... 713 Whitmarsh Lane

LAKE CITY

Bill Rivers Restaurant .... 931 Taylor Street
Mrs. B. J. Jones Tourist Home .... 720 E. Leon Street
Mrs. M. McCoy Tourist Home .... 730 E Leon Street
Rivers Tourist Home .... 931 Taylor Street

LAKELAND

Mrs. A. Davis Tourist Home .... 518 West 1st Street
Mrs. J. Davis Tourist Home .... 842½ N. Fla. Avenue
Rainey's Tourist Home .... 152 Lake Beulah Dr.

MIAMI

Booker T. Motel .... 4200 N.W. 27th Ave.
Dorsey Hotel .... 941 N.W. 2nd Ave.
Hampton House .... 4200 N.W. 27th Ave.
Leonard's Bakery .... 1655 N.W. 3rd Ave.
Mary Elizabeth Hotel .... 642 N.W. 2nd Ave.
Miami-Carver Hotel .... 899 N.W. 3rd Ave.
Sir John Hotel .... 276 N.W. 6th St.

SOUTH MIAMI

Alexander & Sons Grill .... 6454 S.W. 59th Place

OCALA

The Brown Derby .... 902 Lincoln St.

OPA LOCKA

Grant's Drive Inn .... 15055 N.W. 22nd Ave.
Bunche Park Service Station .... 15525 N.W. 22nd Ave.
Stewart's City Service Garage .... 14585 N.W. 22nd Ave.

ORLANDO

Brigg's Restaurant & Rooming House .... 619 & 619½ S. Parramore St.
Sun-Glo Motel .... 737 So. Orange Blossom Trail
Wells Bilt Hotel .... 509 W. South Street
Coleman's Cross Country Gas Station .... cor. Ivey Lane & Gore Ave.

PERRINE

J. J.'s Gulf Service .... 17690 Homestead Avenue

PLANT CITY

Chat & Chew .... 420 Laura Street

POMPANO BEACH

Kidd's Place .... 745 Hammond Road
Ali's Hotel & Bar .... 312 N.W. 6th Avenue
Hotel Grisham .... 407 N.W. 4th Avenue

RICHMOND HEIGHTS

Mondell Gulf Service .... 14600 Lincoln Blvd.

RIVIERA BEACH

Davis Bros. Garage .... 819 Old Dixie Highway
Ebony Motel .... 1101 Old Dixie Highway

ST.AUGUSTINE

F. M. Kelly Tourist Home .... 83 Bridge Street

ST. PETERSBURG

Club Moton .... 642 22nd Street, South
Seymoure Service Station .... 1079 3rd Avenue, South

TALLAHASSEE

Abner—Virginia Motel .... Bragg Dr. at Railroad Avenue

TAMPA

Afro Hotel .... 722 La Salle Street
Anthony's Drive Inn .... 1501 Main Street
Anthony's Coffee Shop .... 720 La Salle Street
Pyramid Hotel .... 1028 Central Ave.

WEST PALM BEACH

West Virginia Hotel .... Cor. 3rd & Sapodilla Ave.
Palm Garden Drug Store .... 332 Rosemary Avenue

GEORGIA

Hotels — Motels — Tourist Homes — Restaurants

ADRIAN

Wayside Tourist Home .... U. S. Route 80

ATLANTA

Connally Tourist Home .... 125 Walnut Street, S.W.
Forrest Arms Hotel .... 325 Butler Street, N.W.
Henry's Grill & Lounge .... 180 Auburn Avenue
Hotel Royal .... 214 Auburn Avenue, N.E.
Joe's Coffee Bar .... 200 Auburn Avenue
Mack Hotel .... 548 Bedford Place, N.E.
Paramount Grille .... 688 East Avenue, N.E.
Paschal Bros. Restaurant .... 837 Hunter Street, N.W.
Savoy Hotel .... 239 Auburn Avenue, N.E.
★STRATTON'S TEA ROOM .... 2991 Peachtree Rd.
Waluhaje Hotel .... 239 W. Lake Avenue, N.W.
Y.M.C.A. .... 22 Bulter Street
Haugabrook's Funeral Home .... 364-66 Auburn Avenue, N.E.

AUGUSTA

Crimm's Hotel .... 725 9th Street
Foster Tourist Home .... 1110 12th Street
Paramount Motel

BRUNSWICK

Melody Tourist Inn .... 1403 G Street
The Palms Tourist Home .... 1309 Glouster Street

CHICKAMAUGA, GA.

C. D. Halerig & Sons .... R.F.D. 2

COLUMBUS

Carver Heights Motel .... Rigon Road
Lowe's Hotel .... 724 5th Avenue
Miles Auto Wrecking .... 1807 Cussetta Road
Y.M.C.A. .... 521 9th Avenue

DOUGLAS

Economy Hotel .... Cherry Street
Lawson's Tourist Home .... Pearl Street
Thomas' Restaurant .... Pearl Street

DUBLIN

Dudley's Motel & Cafe .... 505 E. Jackson (U.S. 80)
Mrs. R. Hunter Tourist Home .... 504 S. Jefferson Street

EASTMAN

J. P. Cooper Tourist Home .... 211 College Street

JEKYLL ISLAND

DOLPHIN CLUB & MOTOR HOTEL .... Jekyll Island

JESUP

Robinson Motel .... 391 No. 4th Street

MACON

Douglas Hotel .... 373 Broadway
Mabell's Place .... 247 5th Street

Hotel Richmond .... 335 Broadway
Jean's Restaurant .... 545 Cotton Avenue

MARIETTA

East Side Cab Stand .... 399 N. Fairground Street
Hunter's Lunch & Lounge .... 501 Hunt Street

PERRY

Ebony Motor Court .... U. S. Hwy. 41 South

SAVANNAH

Blay Boy Motel .... 52nd St. Exit
Southside Motel .... Rt. 17 Ogeecheer, 1/2 Mile

STATESBORO

Gross Motel

THOMASVILLE

Imperial Hotel .... Tallahassee Highway

VALDOSTA

Mae's Tourist Home .... 414 North Street

WAY CROSS

Paradise Restaurant .... Oak Street

HAWAII

Hotels — Motels — Tourist Homes — Restaurants

HILO

Hilo Hotel .... 142 Kinoole St.
Lanai Motel .... 103 Banyan Dr.
Naniloa Hotel .... 495 Kilohana St.

HONOKAA

Honokaa Club Hotel .... P. O. Box 185

KAILUA-KONA

King Kamehameha Hotel
Kona Inn .... Kailua Bay

Island of Kauai

HANALEI

Hanalei Plantation

LIHUE

Coco Palms Resort Hotel
Kauai Inn

Island of Maui

HANA

Hana-Maui Resort Hotel
Sheraton-Maui Hotel

Island of Oahu

HONOLULU

Aina Luana Apartment Hotel .... 358 Royal Hawaiian Ave.
Ala Koa Apartment Hotel .... 2439 Koa Ave.
Ala Moana Ebbtide Hotel .... 1920 Ala Moana

Sutherland Hotel .... 47th & Drexel Blvd.
The Corner .... 111th & Vincennes (Morgan Park)
The Place .... 619 East 63rd Street
Tippin-Inn Lounge .... 325 East 35th Street
Trocadero Lounge .... 4719 Indiana
Vel-Mar Hotel .... 2120 W. Washington St.
★**WEDGEWOOD TOWERS HOTEL .... 6401 So. Woodlawn Ave.**
Y.M.C.A. .... 500 S. Indiana Avenue

CARBONDALE

Plaza Court .... 600 E. Main Street

DANVILLE

Just—A—Mere Hotel .... 218 East North Street

EAST ST. LOUIS

38 CLUB .... 34th & St. Clair Sts.
Bond Food Shop .... 628 Bond Street
Bush's Rib Station .... 1836 Missouri Avenue
Hotel Harlem .... 1426 Broadway
Mid-Town Service Station .... 1501 Broadway
Murray's Standard Service .... 3765 Bond Avenue
Nichol's Drive Inn .... 900 Missouri Avenue
Rock Grill .... 1433 Brady

PEORIA

Wind's Motel .... 3527 W. Harmon Way
★**MRS. CLARA EUBANK'S TOURIST HOME .... 741 N. Monson Street**

ROCKFORD

Briggs Hotel .... 429 Court Street
Mrs. Brown Tourist Home .... 927 S. Winnebago Street
Mrs. C. Gorum Tourist Home .... 301 Steward Avenue
S. Westbrook Tourist Home .... 630 Lexington Avenue

SPRINGFIELD

Dr. Ware Tourist Home .... 1520 E. Washington Street
Mrs. B. Mosby Tourist Home .... 1614 E. Jackson Street
Mrs. Bernie Eskridge Tourist Home .... 1501 Jackson Street
Mrs. G. Bell Tourist Home .... 625 No. 2nd Street
Mrs. L. Jones Tourist Home .... 1230 East Jefferson Street

VIENNA

McCormick Motel .... Highway 45 & 146, 1/2 Mile So. of Vienna

INDIANA

Hotels — Motels — Tourist Homes — Restaurants

ANGOLA

Pryor's Lodge .... East Side Fox Lake Resort, RR 2
The Mar-Fran Motel .... U. S. 20, 1 mi. West of Angola, then 1/2 mi. So.

ELKHART

Miss E. Botts Tourist Home .... 336 St. Joe Street

EVANSVILLE

Hotel Rena .... 661 Governor Street
Mrs. H. Best Tourist Home .... 658 Lincoln Avenue

FRANKLIN

Tanyika Inn .... 751 W. King Street

FORT WAYNE

Howell Hotel .... 1803 S. Hanna Street
Mrs. B. Talbot Tourist Home .... 456 E. Douglas
Stewart's Restaurant .... 621 E. Brackenridge Street
West Acres Motel .... 1301 Goshen Avenue

GARY

★HOTEL TOLEDO .... **22nd Avenue & Adams Street**
Hayes Hotel .... 2167 Broadway

INDIANAPOLIS

Blue Eagle Restaurant .... 701 Indiana Avenue
Foster Hotel .... 2154 N. Illinois Street
Guest House .... 31 West 22nd Street
Perkins Restaurant .... 793 Indiana Avenue
Severin Hotel .... 201 So. Illinois Avenue
Trade Winds Motel .... 2922 Madison Avenue
Y.M.C.A. .... Senate Avenue Branch
Y.M.C.A. .... 806 W. 10th Street
Y.W.C.A. .... 329 N. Penn Street

KOKOMO

Mrs. C. W. Winburn Tourist Home .... 1015 Kennedy Street
Mrs. Charles Hardinson Tourist Home .... 812 Kennedy Street
Mrs. S. D. Hughes Tourist Home .... 1045 N. Kennedy Street

LAFAYETTE

Green Acres Motel .... Hwy. 52, North

MARION

Marshal's Restaurant .... 414-418 East 4th Street
Mrs. Albert Ward Tourist Home .... 324 West 14th Street

MICHIGAN CITY

Allen's Tourist Home .... 210 East 2nd Street

MUNCIE

Gray's Motel .... 3600 No. Broadway
Y.M.C.A. .... 9065 Madison Street

SOUTH BEND

Alou Tourist Hotel .... 2261 Dixie Way, North
Smokes Restaurant .... 432 So. Chapin Street

VINCENNES

Grand Hotel .... P. O. Box 118

WEST BADEN SPRINGS

Waddy Hotel

IOWA

Hotels — Motels — Tourist Homes — Restaurants

CEDAR RAPIDS

Brown's Tourist Home .... 818 9th Avenue, S.E.
Sepia Motel .... Mt. Vernon Road, S.E.

CLINTON

Mississippi View Motel .... 2626 Harding

COUNCIL BLUFFS

Grove Motel .... So. Omaha Bridge Rd.
Woodland Echoes Village .... 429 N. 27th

DAVENPORT

Davenport Hotel

DES MOINES

Community Restaurant .... 1202 Center Street
Erma & Carrie's Restaurant .... 1008 Center Street
Maple Grove Motel .... 6500 Hickman Rd.
Peck's Restaurant .... 1180 13th Street
Y.W.C.A. .... 512 9th Street
Sampson Restaurant .... 1246 East 17th Street

DUBUQUE

Canfield Hotel

IOWA CITY

Oak Grove Motel .... Hwy. 6
Skyway Motel .... Hwy. 218, South

NEWTON

Hillcrest Motel .... 3120 1st Ave., E., Hwy. 6

OTTUMWA

Park Hotel .... Box 375
William Bailey Tourist Home .... 526 Center Avenue

SIOUX CITY

Floyd Park Motel .... 2236 Williams Avenue
Prince Henry Restaurant .... 818 Hamilton Street
West Hotel

WATERLOO

Hotel Ellis
Mrs. B. F. Tredwell Tourist Home .... 928 Beach Street
Mrs. E. Lee Tourist Home .... 745 Vinton Street
Mrs. Spencer Tourist Home .... 220 Summer Street
Swing Inn Motel .... 821 Washington

KANSAS

Hotels — Motels — Tourist Homes — Restaurants

ABILENE

Diamond Court Motel .... 1403 N.W. 3rd Street
Sunflower Hotel .... Box 237

ATCHISON

Mrs. M. McDonald Tourist Home .... 1001 South 7th Street

CONCORDIA

Mrs. B. Johnson Tourist Home .... 102 East 2nd Street

DODGE CITY

Shangri-La Motel

EMPORIA

Elliott's Tourist Home .... 816 Congress Street

EDWARDSVILLE

Road House Tourist Home .... Anderson's Hwy., 32 & Bitts Creek

FORT SCOTT

Hall's Hotel .... 223½ East Wall Street
Harrison's Court Motel .... 1916 E. Wall
Todds Motel .... Rt. 69

GARDEN CITY

Trail Inn Court Motel .... Hwy. 50

HIAWATHA

Mrs. Mary Sanders Tourist Home .... 1014 Shawnee

HUTCHINSON

Beauty Rest Motel .... 2927 East 4th Street
Mrs. C. Lewis Tourist Home .... 400 West Sherman

JUNCTION CITY

Bridgeforth Hotel .... 311 East 11th Street

KANSAS CITY

Crown Court Motel .... 4120 State Street
Hale's Court .... 4110 State Street
Y.W.C.A. .... 644 Quindaro Blvd.

LARNED

Carrie's Bar-B-Q Restaurant .... 218 East 4th Street
Mrs. C. M. Madison Tourist Home .... 828 West 12th Street
Mrs. John Caro Tourist Home .... 218 East 4th Street
Mrs. Mose Madison Tourist Home .... 518 West 10th Street

LAWRENCE

Snowden's Hotel .... 1933 Tennessee Street

LEAVENWORTH

Leavenworth Motel .... 2100 So. 4th Street

MANHATTAN

George's Motel .... 826 Yuma Street
Mrs. E. Dawson Tourist Home .... 1010 Yuma Street

SALINA

Canary Motor Court .... 510 No. Broadway

STOCKTON

L. D. Fuller

TOPEKA

Ace Motel .... Junction Hwys. 75-24-40
Ace Motor Court .... 2117 Central
Capitol Hotel .... 105 East 5th Street
F. W. Woolworth Co. Cafeteria .... 627 Kansas Avenue
Mrs. E. Slaughter Tourist Home .... 1407 Monroe
Palma House Hotel .... 1811 W. 8th Street
Pennant Cafeteria .... 915 Kansas Avenue
Purple Cow Coffee Shop .... Box 118
Senate Cafeteria .... 822 Kansas Avenue

WICHITA

Allis Hotel .... Broadway & William Sts.
Lassen Hotel .... E. 1st & Market Streets
Osage Motel .... 3358 S. Broadway

KENTUCKY

Hotels — Motels — Tourist Homes — Restaurants

BOWLING GREEN

Hotel Southern Queen .... State Street, Hwy. 31-w

ELIZABETHTOWN

Mrs. B. Tyler Tourist Home .... 224 No. Niles Street

HOPKINSVILLE

L. McNary's Tourist Home .... 113 Liberty Street
Mrs. E. Davis Tourist Home .... 901 E. Hayes Street

LEXINGTON

Greystone Motel .... Race Street
Huggins Service Center .... 7th & Lime
Mrs. K. Wallace Tourist Home .... 600 W. Maxwell

LOUISVILLE

Brown Derby Lounge .... 563 S. 10th Street
Elite Tavern & Grill .... 2801 W. Walnut
Frank's Service Station .... 729 W. Walnut
Hook's Hotel .... 8th & Chestnut Street
Mickey's Bar & Grill .... 633 S. 10th Street
The Allen Hotel .... 2516 W. Madison Street
Turner's Drive In .... 3671 Newburg Road
Y.M.C.A. .... 920 W. Chestnut Street
Y.W.C.A. .... 206 W. Broadway

MAMMOTH CAVE NATIONAL PARK

Mammoth Cave Hotel .... Open year round

PADUCAH

Jefferson Hotel .... 514 South 8th Street

LOUISIANA

Hotels — Motels — Tourist Homes — Restaurants

ALEXANDRIA

The Orient Hotel .... 725½ Lee Street

BASTROP

Blue Front Cafe .... 423 W. Madison

BATON ROUGE

Ever Ready Hotel .... 1325 Government Street
Ideal Cafeteria .... 1501 E. Boulevard
Lincoln Hotel .... 400 South 13th Street
Pearson's Tourist Home .... 1515 Oleander Street
T. Harrison Tourist Home .... 1236 Louisiana Avenue

KENNER

Tanner's Motel .... Rte. 1, Box 1096

LAFAYETTE

Bourges Tourist Home .... 416 Washington Street

LAKE CHARLES

Combre's Place Tourist Home .... 601 Boulevard
Grand Terrace Hotel .... 531 Boulevard
Lewis Hotel .... 515 Boulevard

MONROE

Blue Moon Restaurant .... 1811 Conover Street
Crane's Hotel .... 503 Adams Street
Dudley's Hotel .... Desiard Street
Nelson's Motel ....
Red Union Restaurant .... 705½ Desiard Street

MORGAN CITY

Mrs. L. Williams .... 719 Federal Avenue
Mrs. V. Williams .... 208 Union Street

NEW ORLEANS

Astoria Hotel .... 235 So. Rampart Street
Caladonia Inn Hotel .... St. Claude & St. Phillip
Dooky Restaurant .... Cor. Orleans & Miro
Foster's Chicken Den Restaurant .... Cor. LaSalle & 7th Sts.
Gladstone Hotel .... 3435 Dryades Street
Golden Leaf Hotel .... 1209 Saratoga Street
Gumbo House Restaurant .... 1936 Louisiana Avenue
Harris House Hotel .... 1383 St. Bernard Avenue
Honey Dew Inn Restaurant .... 115 Front Street
Hotel Foster .... 2926 LaSalle Street
Marsalis Motel .... 110 Shrewsbury Road
★**MASON'S MOTEL** .... **3923 Melpomene Street**
Mrs. J. Montgomery Tourist Home .... 2134 Harmony
Mrs. King Tourist Home .... 2826 Louisiana Avenue
Mrs. P. Robinson Tourist Home .... 9038 Olive Street
N. J. Bailey Tourist Home .... 2426 Jackson Avenue
North Side Hotel .... 1518 La Harpe Street
Place-Of-Joy Restaurant .... 2700 Melpomene Street
Portia's Restaurant .... 2426 Louisiana Avenue
Riley's Guest House .... 1983 N. Rocheblave Street
Robin Hood Hotel .... 2132 Simon Bolivar Street
Robinson's Tourist Home .... 3300 Hamilton Street
Shadowland Hotel .... 1921 Washington Avenue
Vogue Hotel .... 1116 N. Dorgenois Street
Roosevelt Haney .... 2112 Felicity Street

NEW IBERIA

M. Robertson Tourist Home .... 116 Hopkins Street
N. E. Cooper Tourist Home .... 913 Providence Street

OPELCUSAS

B. Giron Tourist Home .... 510 So. Lombard Street

SHREVEPORT

Castle Hotel .... 1000 Sprague Street
George Washington Carver Branch Y.M.C.A. .... 1051½ Texas Avenue
Hollywood Cities Service Station .... 3807 Hollywood
King's Circle Inn Bar-B-Que .... 4054 Miles
Lloyd's Hotel .... 1229 Milan Street
Mrs. A. Harris Tourist Home .... 2848 Milan Street
Mrs. Ed. Turner Tourist Home .... 309 Douglas Street
Sprague Hotel .... 1032 Sprague Street
The New Airport Motel .... 4416 Hollywood
Will Steward Hotel .... 1249 Oakland

WEST MONROE

Jackson's Motel .... 2004 Cypress Street
Myles' Auto Parts & Wrecking Co. .... 2122 Cypress Street

MAINE

Hotels — Motels — Tourist Homes — Restaurants

BANGOR

THE BANGOR HOUSE Motor Hotel .... Main at Union Streets

Downtown Bangor, Family Plan, TV, AAA, Duncan Hines, Dining Room,
Coffee Shop & Cocktail Lounge — Tel Ban 7321

DIXFIELD

Marigold Motel .... Hwy. 2, 10 Miles East of Rumford

OLD ORCHARD

Mrs. R. Cumming's Tourist Home .... 110Portland Avenue

PORTLAND

Thomas House Tourist Home .... 28 "A" Street
Swampscotta Lodge........ Rt. 302, 9 miles from Portland

ROBBINSTON

Brook's Bluff Cottage .... Hwy. 1, 12 Miles East of Calais

MARYLAND

Hotels — Motels — Tourist Homes — Restaurants

ANNAPOLIS

Alsop's Restaurant .... Northwest & Calvert Sts.
Brown Hotel .... 50 Clay Street

BALTIMORE

Club Bargeque .... 1519 Penn. Avenue
Honor Reed Hotel .... 667 No. Franklin
Majestic Hotel .... 1602 McCulloh Street
Sphinx Restaurant .... 2107 Pennsylvania Avenue
Sess Restaurant .... 1639 Division Street
Spot Bar-B-Q Restaurant .... 1530 Penn. Avenue
White Rice Inn .... 1306 Penn. Avenue
Y.M.C.A. .... 1617 Druid Hill Avenue
Y.W.C.A. .... 1916 Madison Avenue

BOWIE

Stephen Bowie Hotel .... Bowie-Laurel Road

ELKRIDGE

Bass Motel .... U. S. Rt. No. 1

FAULKNER

Blue Star Motel .... Rt. 301, 6 miles N. of Potomac River Bridge

FREDERICK

Crescent Restaurant .... 16 W. All Saint Street
Mrs. J. Makel Tourist Home .... 119 East 5th Street
Mrs. W. W. Roberts Tourist Home .... 316 W. South Street

HAGERSTOWN

Harmon Tourist Homes .... 226 N Jonathan Street
Ship Tea Room .... 329 N. Jonathan Street

HAVRE DE GRACE

Johnson's Hotel .... 415 So. Stokes Street

SALISBURY

Franklin Hotel .... U. S. Hwy. 50, 6 blocks W. of Rt. 13

WALDORF

Blue Jay Motel .... U. S. 301

MASSACHUSETTS

Hotels — Motels — Tourist Homes — Restaurants

BOSTON

Bedford Motel........ Rt. 4, Exit #36, Off Rt. 128
Charlie's Restaurant .... 429 Columbus Avenue
Columbus Arms Hotel .... 455Columbus Avenue

Harriet Tubman Hotel .... 25 Holyoke Street
Holeman Tourist Home .... 212 W. Springfield Street
Julia Walters Tourist Home .... 912 Fremont
M. Johnson Tourist Home .... 616 Columbus Avenue
Mrs. E. A. Taylor Tourist Home .... 192 W. Springfield Street
Slades Restaurant .... 958 Tremont Street
Sunnyside Restaurant .... 411 Columbus Avenue
The Manger .... Causeway & Nashua Streets
Western Restaurant .... 415 Mass. Avenue

BUZZARDS BAY P.O.

Wagon Wheels .... Savary Avenue, R.F.D.

CAMBRIDGE

Mrs. S. P. Bennett Tourist Home .... 26 Mead Street

GREAT BARRINGTON

Mrs I. Anderson Tourist Home .... 28 Rossiter Street
Mrs. J. Hamilton Tourist Home .... 118 Main Street

HYANNIS

Cape Traveler Motel .... Rt. 28, 2 miles east of Hyannis
Zilphas Cottages Tourist Home .... 134 Oakneck Road
Hyannisport .... Hilltop, P. O. Box 205

KINGSTON

Kingston Inn .... Kingston, Mass.
Camp Twin Oaks .... Tel. Kingston 468

NANTUCKET ISLAND

The Skipper Restaurant

NORTH CAMBRIDGE

Mrs. L. G. Hill Tourist Home .... 39 Hubbard Avenue

OAK BLUFFS

Brownie's Cottage .... P. O. Box 788
Cinderella Cottage .... 36 Pequot Avenue
Dunmere-By-The-Sea .... 5 Penacock Avenue
Maxwell Cottage .... P. O. Box 1354
O'Brien House .... 220 Circuit Avenue
Oliver W. Moody .... Box 327
Scott's Cottage .... P. O. Box 1131
Shearer Cottage ....

PITTSFIELD

J. Marshall Tourist Home .... 124 Danforth Avenue
M. E. Grant Tourist Home .... 53 King Street
Mrs. T. Dillard Tourist Home .... 109 Linden Street

PROVINCETOWN

Kalmar Village .... Rt. 6

RANDOLPH

Chickenshack .... 428 Main Street

SPRINGFIELD

Hotel Springfield .... 1827 Main Street

MICHIGAN

Hotels — Motels — Tourist Homes — Restaurants

ANN ARBOR

Allenel Hotel .... 126 El Huron Street
American Hotel .... 123 Washington Street

BATTLE CREEK

Mrs. F. Brown Tourist Home .... 76 Walters Avenue

BALDWIN

Whip-Or-Will Cottage .... Rt. No. 1 Box 153

BITLEY

Kelsonia Inn .... Woodland Park
Royal Breeze Hotel .... Woodland Park

CASSOPOLIS

Idlehour Country Club .... Phone: State 2-2834
Caslen's Blue Bell Garden .... Rt. 1
Dagg's Cottage .... Rt. 1
Everett Rest Haven .... Rt. 1
Royal Breeze Hotel .... Rt. 1

DETROIT

Capitol Hotel .... 114 East Palmer
Capri-Plaza Hotel .... 7541 Linwood Street
Ebony Hotel .... 110 Chandler Street
Gotham Hotel .... 111 Orchestra Place
Mark Twain Hotel .... 52 E. Garfield
McGraw Hotel .... 5605 Junction Street
Mt. Royal Hotel .... 8841 Woodward Ave.
Russell Hotel .... 615 E. Adams Street
Summers Hotel .... 412 Frederick Street
Summers Hotel .... 2940 Harding Street
Thomas Hotel .... 244 E. Kirby Street
Town Motel .... 2127 W. Grand Blvd.

FLINT

Elms Park Motel .... 2801 So. Dort Hwy.
Mrs. F. Taylor Tourist Home .... 1615 Clifford Street
T. L. Wheeler Tourist Home .... 1512 Liberty Street

GRAND RAPIDS

Villa Court Motel .... 5451 So. Division

HART

Bryson's Lake View .... 202 N. State Street

IDLEWILD

B. Riddles Tourist Home
Bask Inn Tourist Home .... Broadway at Hemlock
Casa Blanca Hotel
Club El Morocco Hotel .... Rt. No. 1
Douglas Manor Tourist Home
Edinburgh Cottage, Miss Herrons Tourist Home
McKnight's Hotel
Navajo Restaurant
Oakmere Hotel
Paradise Gardens Hotel
Phil Giles Hotel
Rainbow Manor Tourist Home
Rest Haven Tourist Home
Rosanna's Restaurant
Spizerinktom Tourist Home
The Pomiserania Lodge .... Box 815
Whiteway Inn Restaurant

INKSTER

Mona Lisa Motel .... 28725 Michigan Ave.

JACKSON

Mooreman Tourist Lodge .... 1120 So. Milwaukee Street

Mrs. W. Harrison Tourist Home .... 126 Moore

LANSING

Mrs. Gaines Tourist Home .... 1406 Albert Street

Mrs. James Lewis Tourist Home .... 816 S. Butler Street

Sonny's Tropicana Lodge .... Division & Williams Streets

MACKINAW CITY

Parkview Cabins .... 114 Depeyster Street

MUSKEGON

R. C. Merrick Tourist Home .... 65 E. Muskegon Avenue

NEW BUFFALO

Fireside Restaurant .... U. S. Route 12

OSCODA

Jesse Colbath Tourist Home .... Van Eten Lake

PONTIAC

Motel Morocco .... 597 Franklin Rd.

VANDALIA

Copper Motel .... Hwy. M 60, Bet. Chicago & Detroit

Mrs. Mayme Cooper Tourist Home .... P. O. Box 96

THREE RIVERS

Jordan's Tourist Home .... Rt. 4, Box 289

Wilson's Farm .... Rt. 3, Box 196

MINNESOTA

Hotels — Motels — Tourist Homes — Restaurants

AUSTIN

Fox Hotel .... 501 N. Main Street

BENSON

Earl's Motel .... Hwy. 9

DULUTH

London Road Court .... 2521 London Rd.

GRAND RAPIDS

Holiday Village Motel .... Junction U.S. 2 & 169-E

MINNEAPOLIS

Parkway Motor Court .... 4757 Hiawatha Avenue

MOTLEY

Herman Steick's Restaurant

ROCHESTER

Avalon Hotel .... 303 North Broadway

De Luxe Motor Court .... Hwys. 14 & 52

ST. CLOUD

Grand Central Hotel .... 5th & St. Germaine

Kays Motel .... 102 Lincoln Avenue

Spaniol Restaurant .... 13 6th Avenue No.

ST. PAUL

Coleman's Restaurant .... 2239 Ford Parkway

Covered Wagon .... 320 Wabasha

Hotel Lowery .... 339 Wabasha

Hotel Ryan .... 402 Robert

Hotel St. Paul .... 363 St. Peter

Jean's French Restaurant .... 748 Grand
Lee's Village Inn .... 800 Cleveland
Lexington Restaurant .... 1096 Grand
Lindy's Steak House .... 1581 University
Lowry .... 339 Wabasha
Port's Restaurant .... 1046 Grand
Radisson
Ryan .... 6th and Robert Streets
Sarrack Motel .... 946 McKnight Rd.
Sugar's Restaurant .... 201 East 4th Street
Y.M.C.A. .... 123 West 5th Street

WINONA

Hotel Winona
Red Top Motel .... Hwy. 61, West
Winn Tee Pee—Cottage Motel .... Hwys. 61-14-43, ½ Mile East

MISSISSIPPI

Hotels — Motels — Tourist Homes — Restaurants

BILOXI

Mrs. A. J. Alcina Tourist Home .... 443 Washington
Mrs. G. Bess Tourist Home .... 630 Main Street

CLARKSDALE

Riverside Hotel .... 615 S. Sunflower Avenue

COLUMBUS

Mrs. Chevis Tourist Home .... 1425 11th Avenue N.
M. J. Harrison Tourist Home .... 915 N. 14th Street
Queens City Hotel .... 15th Street & 7th Avenue

FOREST

The Sky Way Motel .... Mrs. Guise, Prop., Box 53

GREENVILLE

El Moroco Hotel .... 1039 Nelson Street
Hotel Montrol .... Nelson Street

HATTIESBURG

Crosby's Hotel .... 512 Mobile Street
Mrs. A. Crosby Tourist Home .... 413 E. 6th Street
Mrs. S. Vann Tourist Home .... 636 Mobile Street
W. A. Godbolt Tourist Home .... 409 E. 7th Street

HOLLY SPRINGS

Clark's Dairy Bar & Taxi Service .... On Hiway 78N
College Court Motel .... U. S. Hwys. 78 & Miss. 7

JACKSON

Edward Lee Hotel .... 144 W. Church Street
Summers Hotel .... 619 W. Pearl Street

LAUREL

Mrs. S. G. Wilson Tourist Home .... 806 So. 7th Street

McCOMB

De Soto Hotel .... 601 Summit Street
White Castle Hotel .... Highway 51

MERIDIAN

Beales Hotel .... 2411 Fifth Street
Charley Leigh Tourist Home .... 1425 Fifth Street
Hotel E. F. Young, Jr. .... 500 25th Avenue
Hotel Henderson .... 2507 5th Street

MOUND BAYOU

Leggette's Fan-Cee Freeze .... On Highway 61
Marzel Motel
Mrs. Charlotte Strong Tourist Home
Mrs. Sallie Price Tourist Home

NATCHEZ

Mrs. S. Miller Tourist Home .... 31 Bishop Street
Riverside Restaurant .... 200 S. Broadway

NEW ALBANY

S. Drewery Tourist Home .... Church Street

HOWARD'S MOTEL & SNACK BAR —
540 Oak Street
New Albany, Miss.

Room Rate $1 - $7.50 per night
Night Phone: 634-5829
Day Phone: 534-5829

PASSAGOULA

Mrs. Milline B. Wilson Tourist Home .... 1001 Kenneth Avenue
Jabo's Motel & Restaurant .... 706 E. Live Oak Street

TOUGALOO

Zebra Motel .... Hwy. 51, By Pass, 7 miles N. of Jackson

VICKSBURG

Y.M.C.A. .... 923 Walnut Street

YAZOO CITY

Mrs. A. J. Walker Tourist Home .... 321 S. Monroe

MISSOURI

Hotels — Motels — Tourist Homes — Restaurants

CAPE GIRARDEAU

J. Randol Tourist Home .... 422 North Street
W. Martin Tourist Home .... 38 N. Hanover Street

COLUMBIA

Austin House Hotel .... 1 West Ash Street
Williams Tourist Home .... 110 Lynn Street

EXCELSIOR SPRINGS

Moore's Hotel .... Main Street

HANNIBAL

Mrs. E. Julius Tourist Home .... 1218 Gerard Street

JACKSON

Eulinberg's Place .... U.S. Hiway 61, 14 Mi. of Jackson

JEFFERSON CITY

Blue Tiger Restaurant .... Chestnut & E. Atchenson Street
Booker T. Hotel
Lincoln Hotel .... 600 Lafayette Street
Miss C. Woodridge Tourist Home .... 418 Adams Street

KANSAS CITY

Annabelle's Beauty Nook .... 2306 E. 12 Street
Broyles Brothers Auto Service .... 3031 Prospect
Drumm's Cleaners & Dyers .... Prospect at 35 St.
Eddie's Hickory House .... 17th & Vine
Gather Inn .... 1734 E. 31 Street
Gill-Hodges Pharmacy .... 1512 N. 5th Street
Gladyes Briscoe's Beauty Salon .... 1800 N. 5th Street
Ideal Barber Shop .... 1308 N. 5th Street

Jacqulyn's Cleaners & Launderers .... 29th & Treost
Katz Drug Co.
Last Round-Up .... 1611 E. 12 Street
Levell's Pharmacy .... 1101 Quindaro
Lincoln Hotel .... 13th & Woodland St.
Lock's Beauty Salon .... 3401 Prospect
Lou's Pharmacy .... N.E. Cor. 31st & Brooklyn
M & T Restaurant .... 2013 E. 12th Street
Mardi Gras Night Club .... 19th & Vine
Marmadell's Beauty Salon .... 2118 E. 39th Street
Martha's Cafe .... 1406 N. 5th Street
Mattie's Dinette .... 1820 N. 7th
Melody Lanes Bowling Alley .... 41st & Indiana
Mim's Cafe .... 1603 E. 12th Street
Mr. Burger Drive-In .... 81230 Santa Fe
Mr. J's Beauty Salon .... 2108 E. 39th Street
Mrs. Vallie Lamb Tourist Home .... 1914 E. 24th Street
921 Hotel .... 921 E. 17th Street
Old Kentucky's Restaurant .... 1221 Brooklyn
Oven Restaurant .... 17th & Vine Streets
Parkview Hotel .... 10th & Paseo
Party House .... 510 E. 31st Street
Santa Fe Discount Drugs .... 2701 Prospect
Smith's Ultra Modern Drug Store .... 3839 Prospect
Square Deal Motel .... 1305 E. 18th Street
Street's Motel .... 1510 E. 18th Street
Y.W.C.A. .... 1908 the Paseo
Lincoln Hotel .... 13th & Woodland Sts.
M & T Restaurant .... 2013 E. 12th Street
Mim's Cafe .... 1603 East 12th Street
Mrs. Vallie Lamb Tourist Home .... 1914 E. 24th Street

MOBERLY

Ralph Bass Tourist Homes .... 517 Winchester Street

ST. CHARLES

Virginia's Bar-B-Q Stand .... 824 Clark Street (Rear)

ST. CLAIR

Mrs. L. Hilliard Motel .... U. S. Hiway 66

ST. LOUIS

Abernathy's Adams Hotel .... 4295 Olive Street
Alcorn Hotel .... 4165 Washington Avenue
Anderson's Service Station .... 4950 Northland Pl.
Atlas Hotel .... 4267 Delmar
Booker T. Washington Hotel .... 3930 N. Kings Highway
Collin's Service Station .... 4190 Delmar
Gordon's Rib Station .... 4269 Delmar
Lucille's Food Shop .... 4401 Aldine Street
Northside Grill .... 347 Peardon Drive
Poro Hotel .... 4300 St. Ferdinand Avenue
Sara-Lou Cafe .... 4069 St. Louis Avenue
St. Louis Service Station .... 1906 Whittier Street
West End Hotel .... 3900 W. Beele Street
Wilke's Eat Shop .... 4664 Fairlin Avenue

SPRINGFIELD

Alberta's Hotel .... 617 No. Benton

MONTANA

Hotels — Motels — Tourist Homes — Restaurants

BILLINGS

General Custer Hotel

Rimrock Lodge .... 1200 No. 27th Street

BUTTE

Ham's Court .... 3702 Harrison Avenue

GREAT FALLS

Motel Central .... 715 Central Ave., West

GLACIER NATIONAL PARK

All Hotels Open — June 15 to Sept. 15

Glacier Park Hotel

Porter's De Luxe Cabins .... Hwy. 2

HELENA

Capitol Court .... 1150 11th Avenue

Placer Hotel .... Helena, Montana

LIVINGSTON

Murry Hotel .... 201 West Park

Willow Park Cottages .... U. S. 89

Yellowstone Motel .... So. Main Street

MISSOULA

Hotel Florence

NEBRASKA

Hotels — Motels — Tourist Homes — Restaurants

AINSWORTH

Midwest Hotel

Skinner's Cabins

CHARDRON

Oak's Court Motel .... West Hwy. 20

FREMONT

Gus Henderson Tourist Home .... 1725 N. Irving Street

Shady Nook Cabins .... P. O. Box 45

LINCOLN

Deluxe Court .... 4433 No. 70th Street

Lincoln Hotel .... 9th & "P" Streets

OMAHA

Broadview Hotel .... 2060 N. 19th Street

Patton's Hotel .... 2425 Erskine Street

SCOTTSBLUFF

Eagle's Restaurant .... 1603 Broadway

Welsh Roome Hotel .... 1015 9th Avenue

SIDNEY

Long Pine Court .... 1701 Illinois

VALENTINE

Hotel Marion

NEVADA

Hotels — Motels — Tourist Homes — Restaurants

BOULDER CITY

Boulder Dam Hotel

Lake Meade Lodge

ELKO

★LOUIS MOTEL .... West Elko, Hwy. 40
Phone RE 8-6188 — Family Units — No Pets

LAS VEGAS

Carver House .... Jackson and "D" Streets
Hotel Jackson .... 405 W. Jackson Street
Shaw Apt. Tourist Home .... 619 Van Buren Street
West Motel .... 950 Bonanza Road

RENO

Hawthorne Tourist Home .... 542 Valley Road
New China Club .... 260 Lake Street

NEW HAMPSHIRE

Hotels — Motels — Tourist Homes — Restaurants

LITTLETON

White Wall Motel .... Rt. 302

MANCHESTER

Floyd Hotel .... 614 Elm Street

NEW LONDON

Twin Lake Village

TWIN MOUNTAIN

The Last Chance Motel .... U. S. Highway 3

WHITEFIELD

Mrs. Homer Mason Tourist Home .... Greenwood Street
Mrs. Wm. Nolan .... Union Street

NEW JERSEY

Hotels — Motels — Tourist Homes — Restaurants

ASBURY PARK

E. C. Yeager Tourist Home .... 1406 Mattison Ave.
Mrs. C. Jones Tourist Home .... 141 Sylvan Ave.
Mrs. V. Maupin Tourist Homes .... 25 Atkins Ave.
Mrs. W. Greenlow Tourist Home .... 1315 Summerfield Ave.
Nellie Tutt's Restaurant .... 1207 Springwood Ave.
Reevy's Hotel .... 135 DeWitt Ave.
Waverly Motel .... 138 DeWitt Ave.
West Side Restaurant .... 1136 Springwood Ave.
Whitehead Hotel .... 25 Atkins Ave.

ATLANTIC CITY

Attucks Hotel .... 1120 Drexel Ave.
Burton's Hotel .... 10 North Delaware Ave.
Carver Hall Hotel .... 500 North Carolina Ave.
Gambrill's .... 501 N. Indiana Ave.
Golden's Restaurant .... 41 North Kentucky Ave.
Hawkin's .... 1114 Baltic Ave.
Hotel McCracken .... 1701 Arctic Ave.
Jamaica Motel .... 1140 Adriatic Avenue
Johnson's Hotel .... 11 North Kentucy Ave.
Jones Cottage .... 1720 Arctic Ave.
Kathryn Guest House .... 1817 Arctic Ave.
Liberty Hotel .... 1579 Baltic Ave.
Lincoln Hotel .... 15 North Indiana Ave.

Livingston's Guest House .... 38 N. Rhode Island Ave.
Murphy Tourist Home .... 234 Virginia Ave.
Newsome's Cottage .... 126 N. Indiana Ave.
PARK PLAZA MOTEL .... Illinois Ave. at Bachrach Blvd.
Phone 348-9131 — 26 modern units — Air Conditioned
Perry's Restaurant .... 1222 Arctic Ave.
R. Brown Tourist Home .... 113 North Pennsylvania Ave.
Randell Hotel .... 1601 Arctic Ave.
Stigare Motel .... Absecon Blvd. & Drexel Ave.
Village Inn .... 1806 Arctic Ave
Villanova Hotel .... 1124 Drexel Ave.
Wash's Sea Food Restaurant .... 710 N. Michigan Ave.
Washington Tourist Home .... 1109 Arctic Ave.
Wright Hotel .... 1702 Arctic Ave.

BELMAR
Sadie's Guest House .... 1304 "E" Street

BELL MEADE
Bell Meade Hotel .... U. S. Route 31

BURLEIGH
Indian Trail Motel .... Indian Trail Road

CAPE MAY
Admiral Arms .... 226 Jackson St.
De Griff Hotel .... 83 Corgie Street
Dot's Guest House .... 230 Jackson St.
Indian Trail Motel .... Rt. No. 2
Richardson's Hotel .... Broad & Jackson Streets
Stiles Tourist Home .... 821 Corgie Street

EGG HARBOR
Allen House Hotel .... 625 Cincinnati Avenue

ELIZABETH
Mrs. T. T. Davis Tourist Home .... 27 Dayton

ESTELLE MANOR
Lake La-Will Motel .... First Avenue

FAIR HAVEN
Robin's Nest Hotel .... 83 Navesink Avenue

LAWNSIDE
Hi-Hat Tourist Home .... White Horse Pike
Inman Hotel .... White Horse Pike

MONMOUTH JUNCTION
Macon's Inn Tourist Home .... Highway Rotue No. 1-26

MONTCLAIR
Y.M.C.A. Tourist Home .... 39 Washington Street
Y.W.C.A. Tourist Home .... 159 Glenridge Avenue

NEPTUNE
Busy Bee Cottage .... 418 Fisher Avenue
Gottling's Restaurant .... 118 Bradley Avenue
Hampton Inn Restaurant .... 1718 Springwood Avenue
Samuel's Restaurant .... 351 Fisher Avenue

NEWARK

Alpine House .... 345 Washington Street
Coleman Hotel .... 59 Court Street
Grand Hotel .... 78 W. Market Street
Park Lane Hotel .... 81 Lincoln Park
Y.M.C.A. .... 52 Jones Street
Y.W.C.A. .... 20 Jones Street

OCEAN CITY

Benning Hotel .... 6th St. & Simpson Ave.
Comfort Hotel .... 201 Bay Avenue
Edna Mae's Tourist Home .... 921 West Avenue

ORANGE

Triangle Restaurant .... 152 Barrow Street
Y.M.C.A. .... 84 Oakwood Avenue
Y.W.C.A. .... 66 Oakwood Avenue

PERTH AMBOY

Lenora Hotel .... 550 Hartford Street

PLEASANTVILLE

Fuller's Motel .... 1401 So. New Road
Garden Spot Tourist Home .... 300 Doughty Road
Lin-Mar Hotel .... 1420 So. New Road, Hwy. 9
Marionette Cottage Tourist Home .... 604 Portland Avenue
Morris Beach .... 401 Bayview Ave.
Virginia Hotel .... 1505 New Road
Virginia Inn Tourist Home .... 1505 S. New Road

RED BANK

Vincents Restaurant .... 263 Shewsbury Avenue

SEA BRIGHT

Castle Inn Restaurant .... 11 New Street

SPRING LAKE BEACH

Laster Cottage .... 419 Morris Ave.

TRENTON

HOTEL DE LAINE — ½ Blk. from Bus Terminal .... 152 Perry Street
Clean Attractive Rooms & Baths
Your Home Away from Home — Phone EX 2-9226
Y.M.C.A. .... 40 Fowler Street

WILDWOOD

Arctic Ave. Hotel .... 3600 Arctic Avenue
Dean's Tourist Home .... 166 W. Young Avenue
Elfra Court Motel .... 119 W. Robert Street
Ivy Hotel .... 436 W. Garfield Avenue
Lilian's Tourist Home .... 134 W. Baker Avenue
Mrs. E. Crawley Tourist Home .... 3816 Arctic Avenue
Poindexter Apts. Hotel .... 106 E. Schellinger Avenue
The Harmon Motel .... 4308 Hudson Avenue
The Marion Hotel .... Arctic & Spencer Avenue
The Norris House .... 107 W. Roberts Avenue

NEW MEXICO

Hotels — Motels — Tourist Homes — Restaurants

ALAMOGORDO

Travelers Court Motel .... Hwys. 54 & 70

ALBUQUERQUE

Aunt Brenda's Restaurant .... 331 53 St., N.W.
Cactus Motel .... 5930 Central Ave., S.W.
Mrs. Kate Duncan Tourist Home .... 331 53 St., N.W.
Mrs. W. Bailey Tourist Home .... 1127 N. 2nd Street

CARLSBAD

Black River Village

DEMING

Darling Courts Motel .... West Hwys. 70 & 40
La Mesa .... 822 W. Soruce Street

LORDSBURG, N. M.

ROSWELL

Apache Lodge .... 1401 So. Main Street
B. Brown .... 313 W. Math.

SANTE FE

El Ray Court .... 2500 Cerellios Road

SANTA ROSE

Will Rogers Court .... Will Rogers Drive

TRUTH OR CONSEQUENCES

Black Range Court .... 711 Date Street

TUCUMCARI

Amigo Motel .... 1823 East Gaynell Avenue
Jones' Rooms Tourist .... Box 1002
Rockett Inn Tourist Home .... 524 W. Campbell Street

VADO

Fullers Motel .... Highway 80

NEW YORK STATE

Hotels — Motels — Tourist Homes — Restaurants

ALBANY

Dorsey's Restaurant .... Cor. Van Trumpet & Broadway
Hotel Broadway .... 603 Broadway
Kenmore Hotel .... 76 Columbia Avenue

BUFFALO

Al Fras Service Station........ William & Michigan Sts.
Art's Lounge .... 1164 Jefferson Ave.
BOB & LOU'S TAVERN .... 925 Jefferson
The Friendly Tavern, Good Food, Pleasant Atmosphere
Bon Ton Oasis Cocktail Lounge........ William St.

Costello Cafe & Hotel .... 605 Michigan Street
Claridge Hotel .... 38 Broadway
Crystal Restaurant .... 534 Broadway
DAIRY ISLE .... 263 Jefferson
The Best In Everything To Eat!
Dennis Snack Bar .... 208 William Street
DUBIEL'S LAS VEGAS RESTAURANT .... 535 Broadway
The Best of Food

TL 6-4154 TL 4-9026

GERALD'S RESTAURANT

Delightful Dinners for Particular People — Open 24 hours

165 Broadway, near Michigan Ave. **Buffalo, N. Y.**

Hickory Tavern .... 352 William
Horseshoe Restaurant .... 212 William Street
J. B.'s Gulf Service Station .... #1 — 419 Broadway, #2 — 120 William
Montgomery Hotel .... 486 Michigan Avenue
MOTHER DEAR'S BAR-B-QUE .... 582 William Street
Perry's Snack Bar .... 360 William Street
Perry's Cleaners .... 368 William Street
Pixie's Bar .... 317 Glenwood Avenue
Pine Grill .... Jefferson Avenue & E. Ferry
THE S & L GRILL .... 264 E. Uticar Street

Phone: TL 2-9827 Wholesome Environment

SAM'S RESTAURANT

Specializing in the Best of Barbecue

534 Broadway **Buffalo, N. Y.**

When Passing Through Buffalo Be Our Guest . . .

THE WILLIAMS HOTEL

9 Sycamore Street TL 2-9319 **Buffalo, N. Y.**

WILLIAMS LIQUOR STORE

206 Seneca Street TL 3-7722 **Buffalo, N. Y.**

Sperry's Tan Tempo Lounge .... 757 Michigan Avenue
STINSON'S LIQUOR STORE .... 134 William Street
We Deliver — TL 3-9000 — William Stinson, Prop.
William Campbell Tourist Home .... 210 Brunswick Street
Texas Red Hot Stand .... 1411 Jefferson Avenue

The New Skateland .... Main & Riley Sts.
Y.M.C.A. .... 585 Michigan Avenue

CASTLETON

Mrs. A. Oliver Tourist Home .... Maple Hill

CENTER BRUNSWICK

Twin Acres Motel .... Highway 7, 6 miles North of Troy

CROTON-ON-HUDSON

Watergate Motel .... Albany Post Rd.

CUDDEBACKVILLE

Paradise Farms
Little Lake Lodge

EAST GREENBUSH

Motel Blue Stone .... P.O. Box 417, 6 mi. East of Albany

ELMIRA

Green Pastures Tourist Home .... 670 Dickinson Street

GLEN FALLS

★McFERSON'S HOTEL .... **52 Glen Street**
Hayes Cottage Tourist Home .... 99 Sanford Street

GODEFROY

Resnick's Motel

GREENWOOD LAKE

La Part Cabins
Farm Lake House
Jus Haven
Mrs. Louise Taylor .... P. O. Box 314

HIGH FALLS

Glove Valley Dude Ranch
Wickie Wackie Club

HYDE PARK

Dutch Patroon Garden Hotel St. .... Rt. 9, 4 miles north Pokips

JAMESTOWN

Mrs. I. W. Herald Tourist Home .... 511 W. 10th Street

KERHONKSON

Rainbow Acres
Pegleg Bates

KINGSTON

Gordon Hotel .... 3 Canal Street
Lang's Ranch .... Rte. 4, Morgan Hill Lodge, Tel. Federal 8-9664

LACKAWANNA

GREEN'S RESTAURANT .... **25 Gates Ave.**
Old Fashioned Home Cooking & Barbecue

LAKE GEORGE

Woodbine Cottage .... 75 Deskau Street
Georgian Motel .... U. S. 9, in Lake George Village

LAKE HUNTINGTON

Sister Lillian Resort, Villa Theresa

LAKE PLACID

Dreamland Cottage .... 41 McKinley Street
Camp Parkside .... Woodland Terr.

LARCHMONT

Larchmont Motel .... 50 Boston Rd.

MECHANICSVILLE

Green's Tourist Home .... R.F.D. No. i
Comfort Inn

NAPANOCH

Pine Oak Guest House

NIAGARA FALLS

★MRS. ALICE FORD TOURIST HOME .... 413 1st Street
3 Blocks from the Falls
Anchor Motel .... N. Y. 384 & 265
High Light Barber Shop .... 513 Erie Avenue
Hotel Niagara
Hutchinson Tourist Home .... 1050 Center Avenue
Mrs. Brown Tourist Home .... 1202 Haeberle Avenue
Mrs. Eugene Ellis Tourist Home .... 3501 Royal Avenue
Mrs. R. Reynolds Tourist Home .... 419 1st Avenue
Seventos Creamy Day .... 3214 Cleveland Avenue
W. L. Parker Tourist Home .... 627 Erie Avenue

NEW YORK CITY

HOTEL	RATES SINGLE	RATES DOUBLE
Abbey, 151 W. 51 St.	$ 8.50-10.50	$11.50-16.50
Algonquin, 59 W. 44 St.	10.00-13.00	13.00-17.00
Allerton House, 130 E. 57 St.	8.00-10.00	11.00-16.00
America, 145 W. 47 St.	5.00- 7.00	7.00-10.00
Americana, 52nd St. & 7th Ave.	12.00-28.00	16.00-32.00
Arlington, 18 W. 25 St.	5.00- 8.00	6.00-12.00
Astor, 44 St. & Broadway	9.00-18.00	14.00-24.00
Barbizon-Plaza, 106 Central Pk.	9.50-15.00	15.00-23.00
Belmont Plaza, 49 St. & Lexington Ave.	8.50-16.00	14.00-20.00
Biltmore, 43 St. & Madison Ave.	14.95-25.00	18.95-30.00
Buckingham, 101 W. 57 St.	10.50-14.50	12.50-17.50
Claridge, B'way & 44 St.	7.00-10.00	9.00-15.00
Commodore, 42 St. at Park & Lexington Aves.	11.00-19.00	16.00-24.00
Diplomat, 108 W. 43 St.	7.50- 9.00	9.50-12.00
Drive-In Hotel, 75 Macombs Place		
Edison, 228 W. 47 St.	8.50-12.00	13.50-18.50
Empire, 63rd St. & Broadway	7.00-10.00	10.00-16.00
Essex House, 160 Central Pk., So.	16.00-28.00	20.00-28.00
Executive, 37 St. & Madison	12.50-15.50	15.50-19.50
Fifth Avenue, 5th & 9th Sts.	10.00-14.00	15.00-19.00
George Washington, 23 St. & Lexington Ave.	7.00-10.00	11.50-16.00
Gladstone, 114 E. 52 St.	13.00-17.00	17.00-22.00
Governor Clinton, 371 7 Ave.	8.00-14.00	11.00-21.00
Great Northern, 118 W. 57 St.	7.50-11.00	10.50-14.00
Hadson, 1234 B'way	5.00- 8.00	7.00-12.00
Hamilton, 141 W. 73 St.	5.00- 7.00	7.00- 9.00
Henry Hudson, 353 W. 57 St.	7.25-12.00	11.00-18.50
Holiday Inn, 57 St. - 9th & 10th Aves.	13.00-14.00	17.00-18.00
Howard Johnson's Motor Lodge, 51 St. & 8 Ave.	12.00-20.00	14.00-22.00
Kimberly, 203 W. 74 St.	7.00- 9.00	10.00-14.00

King Edward, 120 W. 44 St.	5.50- 8.00		8.00-12.00
Knickerbocker, 120 W. 45 St.	6.00-10.00		9.00-16.00
Lexington, Lexington & E. 48 St.	10.75-15.95		14.95-20.95
Lincoln Square Motor Inn, 155 W. 66 St.	14.00-18.00		14.00-18.00
Mayfair House, 610 Park Ave.	$18.00-20.00		$20.00-24.00
Mayflower Hotel, 15 Central Park W.	14.00-17.00		16.50-19.00
Meurice Hotel, 145 W. 58th St.	10.00-11.00		15.00-16.00
Murray Hill Hotel, 42 W. 35th St	7.00-10.00		10.00-13.00
Nassau Hotel, 56 E. 59th St.	3.00- 5.00		4.00- 6.00
National Hotel, 592 7th Ave.	6.00- 7.00		9.00-10.00
Navarro Hotel, 112 Central Park S.	16.50-22.00		19.50-26.00
New York Hilton, Ave. of the Americas & 53 & 54	14.00-22.00		18.00-29.00
New Yorker, 34th St. & 8th Ave.	9.00-15.00		13.00-21.00
One Fifth Avenue, 1 5th Ave.	13.00-17.00		16.00-20.00
Paramount Hotel, 235 W. 46th St.	7.50-10.50		10.50-15.00
Paris Hotel, 752 West End Ave.	5.00-8.75		7.50-13.50
Park Crescent Hotel, 150 Riverside Dr.	8.00-15.00		11.00-18.00
Park Lane Hotel, 299 Park Ave.	19.00-22.00		25.00-28.00
Park Plaza, 50 W. 77th St.	4.50- 6.00		7.00-10.00
Park Royal, 23 W. 73rd St.	8.00-12.00		10.00-18.00
Park Sheraton Hotel, 870 7th Ave.	8.50-15.50		13.90-19.50
Peter Cooper Hotel, 130 E. 39th St.	14.00-16.00		16.50-18.50
Piccadilly, 227 W. 45th St.	8.00-12.00		11.00-17.00
Pierre Hotel, 2 E. 61st St.	23.00-27.00		28.00-33.00
Plaza Hotel, 5th Ave. at 59th St.	15.00-29.00		20.00-34.00
Plymouth Hotel, 143 W. 49th St.	7.00-10.00		10.00-17.00
President Hotel, 234 W. 48th St.	7.00-10.00		11.00-15.00
Prince George Hotel, 14 E. 28th St.	11.00-13.00		12.00-17.00
Regency Hotel, Park Ave. at 61st St.	22.00-30.00		27.00-36.00
Riviera Congress Motor Inn, 550 10th Ave.	12.00-16.00		16.00-20.00
Roger Smith Hotel, 501 Lexington Ave.	9.00-14.50		13.00-18.50
St. Moritz, 50 Central Pk. S	11.00-18.00		15.00-21.00
Savoy-Hilton, 5th Ave. at 58th St.	13.00-35.00		18.00-35.00
Schuyler Hotel, 57 W. 45th St.	6.00- 9.00		8.00-11.00
Seventy Park Hotel, 70 Park Ave.	12.50-20.00		17.00-24.00
Shelburne Hotel, 303 Lexington Ave.	10.85-13.85		13.85-16.85
Shelton Towers Lexington Ave., 48-49th Sts.	8.85	11.85	17.85
Sheraton Atlantic, 34th St. & Bway	8.75-14.00		13.75-18.00
Sheraton-East, 341 Park Ave.	19.00-26.00		23.00-30.00
Sheraton Motor Inn, 42nd St. & 12th Ave.	11.50-17.00		17.75-21.00
Skyline Motor Inn, 725 10th Ave.	14.00-18.00		14.00-20.00
Stanhope Hotel, 995 5th Ave.	16.00-24.00		20.00-28.00
Statler-Hilton, 401 7th Ave.	11.00-19.00		14.50-25.00
Summit Hotel, E. 51st St. & Lexington Ave.	14.00-28.00		16.00-37.00
Taft Hotel, 7th Ave at 50th St.	8.50-13.75		11.50-19.75

Theresa Hotel, 7th Ave. at 125th St.	10.48-11.48	10.48-12.48
Times Square Motor Hotel, 255 W. 43rd St.	6.00- 8.00	9.00-12.00
Tudor Hotel, 304 E. 42nd St.	6.00-11.00	10.00-17.00
Tuscany Hotel, 39th St. E. of Park Ave.	18.80-24.80	24.80-30.80
Waldorf-Astoria, 301 Park Ave.	10.00-22.00	16.00-32.00
Warwick Hotel, 65 W. 54th St.	14.00-25.00	18.00-29.00
Wellington Hotel, 59th & 56th Sts. at 7th Ave.	7.75-14.75	11.50-19.50
Wentworth Hotel, 59 W. 46th St.	8.00-12.00	10.00-16.00
Westbury Hotel, Madison Ave. at 69th St.	14.00-20.00	18.00-25.00
Westover Hotel, 253 W. 72nd St.	8.00-10.00	10.00-12.00
Windermere Hotel, 666 West End Ave.	7.00-10.00	10.00-12.00
Winslow Hotel, 45 E. 55th St.	8.00-11.00	12.00-15.00
Wolcott Hotel, 4 W. 31st St.	7.00- 9.00	10.00-14.00
Woodstock Hotel, 127 W. 43rd St.	6.50- 9.00	10.00-14.00
Woodward Hotel, 210 W. 55th St (Broadway)	5.00-8.00	8.00-12.00
Wyndham Hotel, 42 W. 58th St.	11.00-13.00	12.00-14.00
Y.M.C.A. Wm. Sloane House, (Men Only) 356 W. 34th St.	7.50	
The Bronx		
Bronx Park Motel, 2500 Crontona Ave.	12.00	14.00-16.00
Concourse Plaza Hotel, 900 Grand Concourse	7.50-10.00	13.00-19.00
Deegan Motel, 3600 Bailey Ave.	10.00-12.00	12.00-20.00
Riverdale Motor Inn, 6355 Broadway	12.00-14.00	14.00-16.00
Stadium Motor Lodge, W. 167th St.-Major Deegan Expwy.	10.00-12.00	14.00-16.00
Town & Country Motor Lodge, 2244 Tillotson Ave	11.00-13.00	13.00-17.00
Van Cortlandt Motel, 6393 Broadway	8.00-10.00	10.00-14.00
Brooklyn		
Franklin Arms Hotel, 66 Orange St.	6.50- 7.00	8.50-10.00
Golden Gate Motor Inn, Belt Pkwy.-Knapp St.	11.00-13.00	15.00-19.00
Granada Hotel, Lafayette Ave. & Ashland Pl.	8.50-12.00	11.00-16.00
Gregory Hotel, 8315 4th Ave.	8.00	10.00-11.00
Manhattan Beach Hotel, 156 West End Ave.	7.50-16.50	10.00-22.00
St. George Hotel, 51 Clark St.	6.50-14.00	10.00-17.00
Sea Isle Motor Inn, 3900 Shore Pkwy. (Ex. 14 Belt Pkwy)	12.00-18.00	14.00-22.00
Towers Hotel, 25 Clark St.	7.00- 8.00	10.00-13.00
Queens		
Beach Haven Hotel, 243 Beach 19th St., Far Rockaway 91, N. Y.	10.00	15.00-18.00
Crossway Airport Inn At La Guardia, 100-30 Ditmars Blvd., Flushing 69, N. Y.	14.00-18.00	18.00-24.00
Crossway Idlewild Inn, 152-25 138th Ave., Jamaica 34, N. Y.	14.00-15.00	18.00-19.00
Forest Hills Inn, 1 Station Square, Forest Hills 75, N. Y.	8.50-14.00	12.00-20.00
Franklin Hotel, 89-05 163rd St., Jamaica 32, N. Y.	6.00- 8.00	6.00- 9.00
Grand Central Motor Inn, 71-11 Astoria Blvd., Astoria 2, N. Y.	12.00-15.00	15.00-26.00
Homestead Hotel, 82-45 Grenfall St., Kew Gardens 15, N. Y.	9.00-12.00	12.00-15.00

International Hotel, N. Y. Int. Airport, Jamaica 30, N. Y.	12.00-17.00	18.00-22.00
Kew Motor Inn, 80-05 Grand Central Pkwy., Kew Gardens Hills 35, N. Y.	12.00-16.00	16.00-30.00
La Guardia Hotel, 99-11 Ditmars Blvd., E. Elmhurst 69, N. Y.	13.00-17.00	17.00-22.00
Pan American Motor Inn, 79-10 Queens Blvd., Elmhurst 73, N. Y.	15.00-22.00	18.00-28.00
Riviera Idlewild Hotel, N. Y Int. Airport (Belt Pkwy.) Jamaica 30, N. Y.	16.00-20.00	22.00-32.00
Sanford Hotel, 140-40 Sanford Ave., Flushing 55, N Y.	9.00-10.00	13.00-14.00
Schine Inn at Forest Hills, 108-25 Horace Harding Expwy, Flushing 68, N. Y.	12.00-16.00	16.00-18.00
Seaway Idlewild Hotel, N. Y. Int. Airport (Belt Pkwy.) Jamaica 30, N. Y.	16.00-20.00	22.00-32.00
Sheraton-Tenney Inn At La Guardia, 90-10 Grand Central Pkwy., E. Elmhurst 69, N. Y.	12.50-16.50	14.50-20.00
Skyway Hotel, 132-10 S. Conduit Ave., Jamaica 30, N. Y.	13.00-15.00	17.00-22.00
Skyway Hotel La Guardia, 102-10 Ditmars Blvd., Flushing 69, N. Y.	13.00-15.00	17.00-20.00
Sunchester Hotel, 37-52 80th St., Jackson Hts. 72, N. Y.	12.00-14.00	12.00-14.000
Travelers Hotel-Motel, 9400 Ditmars Blvd., (La Guardia Airport), E. Elmhurst 69, N. Y.	13.00	17.00-18.00
Treadway Inn, 114th St. & 37th Ave. (near the Fair) Flushing 52, N. Y.	15.00-17.00	19.00-24.00
Whitman Hotel, 160-11 89th Ave., Jamaica 2, N Y.	9.00-12.00	12.00-15.00
Richmond (Staten Island)		
Richmond Hotel, 71 Central Ave.,	8.40	10.50
Nassau		
Bar Harbour Motel, 5050 Sunrise Hwy. (Rt. 27), Massapequa Park, N. Y.	10.00-11.00	12.00-15.00
Bayberry Great Neck Hotel, 75 N. Station Plaza, Great Neck, N. Y.	13.00	18.00
Bethpage Motel, Hempstead Tpke., Bethpage, N. Y.	10.00-12.00	12.00-20.00
Colony Arms Hotel, 190 Glen Cove Ave., Glen Cove, N. Y.	8.00	11.00-13.00
Colony Hotel, 10 Bond St., Great Neck, N. Y.	9.50-12.00	14.00-18.00
Courtesy Inn Sea-Horse Marina, S. Main St., Freeport, N. Y.	11.00-13.00	12.00-19.00
Farmingdale Motor Lodge, Rt. 110 Broadhollow Rd.), Farmingdale, N. Y.	9.00	10.00-12.00
Garden City Hotel 7th St. & Park Ave., Garden City, N. Y.	12.00-16.00	17.00-21.00
Gateway Motel, Sunrise Hwy., Merrick, N. Y.	12.00-16.00	14.00-18.00
Hempstead Motor Hotel, 130 Hempstead Ave., West Hempstead, N. Y.	12.00-14.00	14.00-20.00
Heritage Quality Court Motor Inn, Jericho Tpke. (Rt. 25), Syosset, N. Y.	11.00-12.00	15.00-19.00
Island Inn, Old Country Rd., Westbury, N Y.	12.00-15.00	16.00-22.00

Island Lodge Motel, 274 Jericho Tpke., Syosset, N. Y.	11.00	16.00-18.00
Jericho Motel, Jericho Tpke., Jericho, N. Y.	9.00-11.00	12.00-20.00
Lynbrook Motor Hotel, 5 Freer St., Lynbrook, N. Y.	12.00-16.00	15.00-30.00
Mansion Hotel, 54 Lincoln Ave., Rockville Cent., N. Y.		
Meadowbrook Motor Lodge, 4400 Jericho Tpke., Jericho, N. Y.	11.00	16.00-18.00
Mineola Hotel, 193 2nd St., Mineola, N. Y.	6.50	8.50-10.00
Promenade Hotel on the beach, 102 W. Broadway, Long Beach, N. Y.	15.00-25.00	25.00-35.00
Raceway Inn Motel, Old Country Rd., at Post Ave., Westbury , N. Y.	12.00-14.00	14.00-18.00
Roosevelt Inn, 1650 Hempstead Tpke., East Meadow, N. Y.	11.00-13.00	14.00-20.00
Roslyn Harbor Hotel, 22 Bryant Ave., Roslyn, N. Y.		
Tivoli Motel, 3400 Brush Hollow Rd., Westbury, N. Y.	12.00	15.00-18.00
Towne & Country Motel, 49 Old Country Rd., Westbury, N. Y.	12.00	15.00-18.00
Turnpike Motel, 434 Hempstead Tpke., W. Hempstead, N. Y.	12.00 15.00	15.00-26.00
Westbury Motel, Jericho Tpke., Westbury, N. Y.	12.00-16.00	12.00-21.00
Orange		
Thayer Hotel, West Point, N. Y.	7.00- 9.00	10.00-12.00
Rockland		
Ashley Motor Court, U. S. Rt. 59, Nanuet, N. Y.		12.00-14.00
Courtesy Inn, N. Y. Thruwy. (Ex. 11), Nyack, N. Y.	11.00-13.00	15.00-19.00
Motel on the Mountain, N. Y. Thruwy (Ex. 15), Suffern, N. Y.	12.00-14.00	17.00-22.00
Pascack Motel, Rt. 59 (N. Y. Thruwy. Ex. 14), Spring Valley, N. Y.	8.00-10.00	10.00-14.00
Suffolk		
Bayshore Inn, 400 Bayshore Rd., Bayshore, N. Y.	11.00-13.00	13.00-16.00
Beacon Motel, Smithtown Bypass & Jericho Tpke., Nesconset, N. Y.	8.00-10.00	12.00
Chevy Chase Motel, 436 Sunrise Hwy., Babylon, N. Y.		10.00-12.00
Eden Rock Motel, 3055 Veterans Memorial Hwy., Ronkonkoma, N. Y.	8.00-12.00	10.00-17.00
Fontenac Motor Lodge, Jericho Tpke.-Bridge Branch Rd., Smithtown, N. Y.	11.00-13.00	14.00-18.00
Huntington Motel, 331 W. Jericho Tpke. (Rt. 25), Huntington, N. Y.	8.00-10.00	10.00-12.00
Jerimac Motel, 2231 Jericho Tpke., Commack, N. Y.	8.00-10.00	10.00-12.00
Lindenhurst Motel, W. Montauk Hwy. & Chestnut St., Lindenhurst, N. Y.	8.00-10.00	10.00-12.00
The 112 Motel, Rt., 112, Medford, N. Y.	8.00-10.00	10.00-14.00
Patchogue Motel & Country Club, Sunrise Hwy. (Rt. 27), Patchogue, N. Y.	8.50	12.00-13.00
Pines Motor Lodge, Rt. 109 near Straight Path, North Lindenhurst, N. Y.	10.00-11.00	10.00-12.00

St. Moritz Motel, Yacht Club Rd., Babylon, N. Y.	12.00-18.00	12.00-18.00
Sky Motel, 7th St. & 3rd Ave. (Rt. 109), N. Lindenhurst, N. Y.	8.00- 9.00	10.00-13.00
Starlite Motel, 760 Little E. Neck Rd. (Sunrise Hwy.), West Babylon, N. Y.	10.00-14.00	10.00-16.00
Three Village Inn, Dock Rd., Stony Brook, N. Y.	6.00	12.00
Walt Whitman Motel, 295 E. Jericho Tpke. (Rt. 25), Huntington St., N. Y.	8.00-10.00	10.00-16.00
Westchester		
Ardsley Acres Hotel Court, 560 Saw Mill River Rd. (Rt. 9A), Ardsley, N. Y.	8.00	12.00-14.00
Central Motel Court, 441 Central Ave., White Plains, N. Y.	9.00	10.00-12.00
Dunwoodle Motor Inn, 300 Yonkers Ave., Yonkers, N. Y.	10.00-12.00	14.00-17.00
Gramatan Hotel, Pondfield Rd., Bronxville 8, N. Y.	8.00-12.00	14.00-18.00
Hawthorne Circle Motor Inn, 20 Saw Mill River Road, Hawthorne, N. Y.	9.00-12.00	11.00-16.00
Hilton Inn, 455 S. Broadway, Tarrytown, N. Y.	12.00-15.00	16.00-20.00
Holiday Inn of Yonkers, 125 Tuckahoe Rd., Yonkers, N. Y.	10.00-14.00	12.00-18.00
Roger Smith Motor Hotel, 1 Chester Ave., White Plains, N. Y.	8.00-13.00	11.50-17.00
Saw Mill River Motel, 25 Valley Rd., Elmsford, N. Y.	10.00-12.00	13.00-17.00
Scarsdale Inn, School La. off Popham Rd., Scarsdale, N. Y.	10.00	15.00
Tarryrest Motel, 542 Tarrytown Rd., White Plains, N. Y.	9.00	11.00-15.00
Trade Winds Motor Court, 1141 Yonkers Ave., Yonkers 2, N. Y.	10.50-12.00	12.00-18.00
Tuckahoe Motel, 307 Tuckhoe Rd., Yonkers, N. Y.	11.00	14.00-15.00
Watergate Motor Hotel, Albany Post Rd. (Rt. 9), Croton-on Hudson, N. Y.	8.00	12.00-14.00
Westchester Town House Motor Inn, 165 Tuckahoe Rd. (N. Y. Thrwy Ex. 6), Yonkers, N. Y.	14.00-16.00	16.00-24.00
Yorktown Motor Lodge, U. S. Rt. 202-Taconic Pkwy., Yorktown Hts., N. Y.	12.00-14.00	14.00-20.00
NEW JERSEY		
Bergen		
Courtesy Inn, Rt. 4, Fort Lee, N. J.	10.00	12.00-20.00
Horizon Motel, U. S. Rt. 46, S. Hackensack, N. J.	10.00-16.00	10.00-22.00
Howard Johnson's Motor Lodge, Rt. 17, Ramsey, N. J.	10.00-12.00	14.00-16.00
Marriott Motor Hotel at Geo Washington Bridge, Hudson Ter. & The Bridge Plaza, Fort Lee, N. J.	10.00-17.00	14.00-25.00
New Orleans Motel, Rt. 4, Fort Lee, N. J.	6.50-11.00	8.00-16.00
Oritani Motor Hotel, 414 Hackensack Ave. (Rt. 4), Hackensack, N. J.	8.00-10.00	10.00-16.00
Palisades Motor Lodge, Rt. 46, Fort Lee, N. J.	8.00	12.00-14.00
Peter Pan Motel, Rt. 3, E. Rutherford, N. J.	8.00-12.00	10.00-16.00
Skyview Motel, Rts. 1 & 9 & 46, Fort Lee, N. J.	9.00-12.00	11.00-13.00

Suburban Motor Hotel, Rt. 4 & Intersection 208, Fair Lawn, N. J.	10.00-12.00	14.00-16.00
Swiss Court Motel, N. J. Hwy. 17, Upper Saddle River, N. J.	7.00- 8.00	9.00-12.00

New York City

THEATRES

Apollo .... W. 125th Street
Astor .... Broadway at 45th Street
Capitol .... 1639 Broadway
Carnegie Hall Cinema .... Seventh Ave. at 57th Street
Criterion .... Broadway at 45th Street
Embassw Newsreel .... 46th Street and Broadway
Guild 50th .... 32 W. 50th Street
Little Carnegie .... 146 W. 57th Street
Palace .... Broadway and 47th Street
Paramount .... Times Square
Plaza .... 58th Street E. of Madison Ave.
Poet's .... 39 W. 54th Street
Radio City Music Hall .... 1260 Sixth Ave.
Rivoli .... 1620 Broadway
Sutton .... 57th Street and 3rd Ave.
Trans-Lux .... 52nd Street on Lexington Ave.
Victoria .... Broadway and 46th Street
Warner .... Broadway and 47th Street

Brooklyn

Al's Restaurant .... 1550 Fulton Street
Caravan Restaurant .... 175 Willoughby Avenue
Dew Drop Restaurant .... 363 Halsey Street
G. & H Restaurant .... 382 Sumner Avenue
Hotel St. George .... 51 Clark Street
La Marchal .... 1200 President Street
Lefferts Hotel .... 127 Lefferts Place
Lincoln Plaza Hotel .... 153 Lincoln Place
Lincoln Terrace Hotel .... 1483 Pacific Street
Little Roxy Restaurant .... 490A Sumner Avenue
Mohawk Hotel .... 379 Washington Avenue
Pleasant Manor Hotel .... 218 Gates Avenue

BARS

La Marchal Supper Club .... 1873 Nostrand Ave., Near President Street

Bronx

Blue Morocco .... 1185 Boston Rd.
Carver Hotel .... 980 Prospect Avenue
Crotona Hotel .... 695 E. 170th Street
Concourse Plaza .... Grand Concourse at E. 161st Street
Fountainhead

NEW ROCHELLE

Harris Restaurant .... 29 Morris Street
Huguenot Hotel .... 242 Huguenot Street
Three 4s .... 444 North Avenue
Week's Restaurant .... 68 Winyah Avenue

New York City

SHOPS AND STORES

From 34 to 59th Street

Macy's	Herald Square
Gimbals	Broadway at 33rd Street
Saks 34th Street	34th Street at Broadway
Altman's	5th Avenue at 34th Street
Lord and Taylor	5th Avenue at 38th Street
Best's	5th Avenue & 51st Street
Bonwit Teller	721 Fifth Avenue
Saks Fifth Avenue	5th Avenue & 49th Street
Tailored Woman	742 Fifth Avenue
Bergdorf Goodman	5th Avenue & 58th Street

IMPORTANT MEN'S SHOP

Wallach's	5th Avenue & 46th Street
Roger's Peet	600 Fifth Avenue, at 48th St.
Weber and Heilbroner	5th Avenue & 47th Street
John David	Broadway & 32nd Street
Browning Fifth Avenue	
Tripler's	366 Madison Avenue
Brooks Bros.	346 Madison Avenue
Saks Fifth Avenue	5th Avenue & 49th Street
DePinna's	650 Fifth Avenue
Abercrombe & Fitch	Madison Avenue & 45th St.
Jarrell John Inc.	518 Fifth Avenue

IMPORTED OR SPECIAL MERCHANDISE

American House (Artistic American handicrafts)	32 E. 52nd Street
Bazaar Francais (Imported kitchen articles)	666 Sixth Ave.
Bonnier's (Scandinavian arts and crafts)	605 Madison Ave.
Delgado's (Latin-American jewelry, textiles)	31 W. 8th Street
Leighton's (Mexican handicraft)	15 E. 8th Street
Irish Industries (Latin and South American decorative objects)	876 Lexington Ave.
Scottish Products (Scotch delicacies, woolens)	24 E. 60th Street
Sweden House (Scandinavian vases, pottery)	12 W. 50th Street
United Nations Gift Shop (Articles from all over the world)	

PARKS, ZOOS, AQUARIUM and GARDENS

Battery Park	Lower Broadway at the Battery
Botanical Gardens	
Bryant Park	42nd St. at 6th Ave.
Central Park Zoo	59th Street to 110th Street
City Hall Park	Broadway and Park Row
Fort Tyron	Myrtle and Nagle Streets
Jacob Riis	Rockaway, Queens
Prospect	Flatbush Ave. and Empire Blvd.
Van Cortlandt	Broadway and 242nd Street
Washngton Square	5th Ave. and 4th Street

POINTS OF INTEREST

- Bowery
- Cathedral of St: John Divine
- Central Park and its Zoo
- Chinatown
- City Hall
- Columbia University
- Coney Island
- Empire State Building
- Freedomland
- Grand Central Terminal
- Grant's Tomb
- Greenwich Village
- Hayden Planetarium
- International Airport
- La Guardia Field Airport
- Lever Building
- Little Italy
- New York Harbor
- Penn Station
- Port Authority Bus Terminal
- Riverside Church
- Rockefeller Center
- Schomburg Collection, Countee Cullen Branch Library
- Statue of Liberty
- Stuyvesant Town
- United Nations
- Wall Street
- Washington Square

RESTAURANTS

Avenue .... 509 Fifth Ave.
Blue Bird Inn .... 121½ E. 17th Street
Bombay Indian .... 465 W. 125th Street
Brass Rails .... 100 Park Ave.
521 Fifth Ave.
745 Seventh Ave.
500 Eighth Ave.
Bus Stop Restaurant .... 21 Macombs Place
Cattlemen's .... 48th St. & Lexington Ave.
China Bowl .... 152 W. 44th Street
Chinese Rathskeller .... 45 Mott Street
Danny's Corner .... 2154 Amsterlam Ave.
Davy Jones Sea Food House .... 103 W. 49th Street
Dawn Cafe .... 1702 Amsterdam Ave.
Eddie's Restaurant .... 714 St. Nicholas Ave.
El Charro .... 4 Charles Street
El Mundial .... 222 W. 116th Street
Frank's .... 315 W. 125th Street
Jack Dempsey's .... 1619 Broadway off 49th Street
King of the Sea .... 879 Third Ave.
Living Room .... 915 Second Ave.
Lobster Box .... 34 City Island Ave.
Lundy's .... 739 St. Nicholas Ave.
Mama Laura .... 230 E. 58th Street
McGinnis .... Broadway at 48th Street
Palm Cafe .... 209 W. 125th Street
Patricia Murphy's Candlelight Rest. .... 33 E. 60th Street
Pete's .... 18 Irving Place
Phil's Rest. .... 187 Third Ave.
Prelude .... 3219 Broadway
Stella D'Oro .... 5806 Broadway
Wells Restaurant .... 2249 7th Ave.
Xochitl Mexican Restaurant .... 146 W. 46th Street

Seafood:

Fisherman's Net .... 495 Third Ave

Grand Central Oyster House .... Grand Central Terminal
Harvey's Seafood House .... 509 Third Ave.
King of the Sea .... 879 Third Ave.
Sea Fare .... 1033 First Ave. also 44 W. 8th Street

Steaks:

Barney's .... 2125 Eighth Ave.
Harlem Embers .... W. 125th Street
Hickory House .... 839 Second Ave.
Lloyd's .... W. 125th Street
Pen and Pencil .... 205 E. 45th Street
Steak Joint .... 58 Greenwich Ave.

American Specialties:

Hearthstone .... 102 E. 22nd Street
Patricia Murphy .... 33 E. 60th Street

Chinese:

House of Chan .... 52nd Street and Seventh Ave.
Ruby Foos .... 240 W. 52nd Street
Lum Fong .... 150 W. 52nd Street

MUSEUMS

American Museum of Natural History .... 79th St. and Central Park West
American Neumismatic Society .... Broadway and 155th Street
Brooklyn .... Washington Ave. and Eastern Parkway
Cloisters .... Fort Tryon Park
Frick Collection .... 5th Ave. and 70th Street
Jewish .... 5th Ave. and 92nd Street
Metropolitan .... 5th and 82nd Street
American Indian .... Broadway at 155th Street
City of New York .... 5th Ave. and 103rd Street
Modern Art .... 11 West 53rd Street
New York Historical Society .... Central West and 77th Street
Solomon R. Gugginheim .... 5th Ave. and 88th Street
Spanish .... Broadway and 155th Street
Whitney .... 22 W. 54th Street

NIGHT CLUBS & BARS

African Room .... 730 Third Ave.
Basin Street .... 137 E. 48th Street
Bell, Cook & Candle .... Amsterdam Ave. at 158th Street
Birdland .... 1678 Broadway
Blue Angel .... 152 E. 55th Street
Bon Soir .... 40 W. 8th Street
Copacabana .... 10 E. 60th Street
Count Basie's .... 2245 Seventh Ave.
Danny's Hide-A-Way .... 151 E. 45th Street
Dawn Cafe .... 1702 Amsterdam Ave.
Dragon Inn .... 140 W. 40th Street
El Morocco .... 307 E. 54th Street
Fireside Inn .... 411 W. 24th Street
Flash Inn .... 107 McCombs Pl.
Gold Brick Inn .... 157th Street & Amsterdam Ave.
Hawaiian Room .... 515 Lexington Ave.
Jimmy Ryan's .... 53 W. 52nd Street
Jock's Place .... 2350 Seventh Ave

La Famille .... 2017 5th Ave.
Linnette's .... 714 St. Nicholas Ave.
Living Room .... 915 Second Ave.
Latin Quarter .... 200 W. 48th Street
Midway Lounge .... 415 W. 125th Street
Nicks' .... 10th Street and Seventh Ave.
Prelude .... 3219 Broadway
Red Rooster .... 2354 Seventh Ave.
Sapphire's .... 271 W. 47th Street
7 Ports .... 1604 Broadway
Smalls' .... Seventh Ave. at 135th St.
Sugar Ray's .... 2074 7th Ave.
Sweet Chariot .... 225 W. 46th Street
The Round Table .... 151 E. 50th Street
Top Club .... 354 W. 125th Street
Upstairs at the Downstairs
and Downstairs at the Upstairs .... 37 W. 56th Street

OSSINING

Depot Square Hotel .... 2 Water Street
Hotel Ossining .... 120 Main Street

PEEKSKILL

B & J Service Station .... Corner Broad & Lincoln Terr.
Greene the Tailor .... 11 Nelson Ave.
Green's Lounge .... Depew Street & Central Ave.
Granberry's .... Park Street
Peekskill Motor Inn .... Rte. 202 Cor. Rte. 9
Towne Lyne Motel .... Rte. 202 Crompond Rd.

PORT JERVIS

R. Pendelton Tourist Home .... 26 Bruce Street

POUGHKEEPSIE

Poughkeepsie Motor Hotel .... Rte. 9

RIVERHEAD

Peter's Motel .... 223 Flanders Road

ROCHESTER

A & A Garage .... 368 Clarissa St.
Arthur's Pharmacy .... 300 Joseph Ave.
Bowers Drug Store .... 553 Plymouth Ave., S.
Gibson Hotel .... 461 Clarissa St.
Headley Dry Cleaners .... 45 South Ave.
La Rue .... 491 Clarissa St.
Lawrence Soda Bar .... 581 S. Plymouth Ave.
Miller's Gulf Service .... Troup and Clarissa
Shamrock Gas & Quaker State Proucts .... 494 South Ave.
Shepard's Barber Shop .... 508 Clinton St., N.
Sol Jeffries Service Station .... 121 Reynolds St.
Stanfield Hotel .... 34 Joseph Ave.

SCHENECTADY

Foster House Hotel .... 310 Dakota Street
Mrs. Grant Thomas Tourist Home .... 1024 Albany

SARATOGA LAKE

White Sulphur Restaurant .... Rte. 9P

SARATOGA SPRINGS

G. & G. Restaurant .... 445 Broadway
Gideon Putnam
James Tourist Home .... 17 Park Street
Mrs. John Parker Tourist Home .... 18 Cherry Street
Playmore Motel .... S. Broadway, Rte. 9
Reds Seafood Restaurant .... Rte. 9

SYRACUSE

Aunt Edith's Restaurant .... 601½ Harrison Street
The Sylvan Tourist Home .... 815 E. Fayette Street
Y.M.C.A. .... 340 Montgomery Street

TARRYTOWN

Hilton Inn .... 455 S. Broadway

TICONDEROGA

Belfred Court .... Corner Montcalm Street & Wayne Avenue

VALATIE

Blue Spruce Motel .... Rt. 9, 16 mi. So. of Albany

WATERTOWN

G. E. Deputy Tourist Home .... 711 Morrison Street
V. H. Brown Tourist Home .... 502 Binase Street
Woodruff Hotel .... Public Square

WHITE PLAINS

Roger Smith Motor Hotel .... 123 E. Post Road
Del Rio Hotel .... 160 Lafayette Avenue
Tarks Restaurant .... 374 Central Avenue
4 Leaf Clover Restaurant .... 70 Dobbs Ferry Road
Waldorf Restaurant .... 102 Grove Street
Winbrook Restaurant .... 136 Brookfield Street
Fields Rotisserie & Motel .... 538 Tarrytown Road

YONKERS

Patricia Murphy's Candlelight Restaurant .... Central Ave.
Trade Winds Motor Ct. .... 1141 Yonkers Ave.

LONG ISLAND

JAMAICA

Boulevard Restaurant .... 110-33 Sutphin Blvd.

ST. ALBANS

Bonvivani Supper Club .... 114-16 Merrick Blvd.
Bowman's Show Place .... 111-59 Farmers Blvd.
Locust Restaurant .... 117-02 Merrick Blvd.
Staghead Club .... 189-29 Linden Blvd.

SPRINGFIELD GARDENS

Club Zanzibar .... 137-08 New York Blvd.

NORTH CAROLINA

Hotels — Motels — Tourist Homes — Restaurants

ASHEVILLE

Booker T. Washington Hotel ..... 409 Southside Avenue
James Keys Hotel ..... 409 Southside Avenue
Mrs. S. Foster Tourist Home ..... 88 Clengman Avenue
Savoy Tourist Homes ..... Eagle & Market Sts.
Y.W.C.A. ..... 194 Ashland Avenue

CHARLOTTE

Addie Motel ..... 516 N. Meyers Street
Alexander Hotel ..... 523 N. McDowell Street
Ingram's Restaurant ..... 304 S. McDowell Street
Alexander's Barber Shop ..... 1310 S. Independence Blvd.
Ballard's Barber Shop ..... Five Points
Biddleville Luncheonette ..... 1116 Beatties Ford Rd.
Chicken 'N' Ribs ..... 1100 Beatties Ford Rd.
Cleanway Cleaners ..... University Park Shopping Center
Davis Sandwich Shop ..... 1108 Spring St.
Ebony Cleaners ..... 318 McDowell St. South
Edith's Snack Bar ..... 716 S. Caldwell St.
Excelsior Club ..... 921 Beatties Ford Rd.
Fairview Barber Shop ..... 1001 Oaklawn Ave.
Ingram's Inn ..... 419 S. Cedar St.
J. C. Hart's Shoe Shop ..... 329 S. McDowell
J. C. Sandwich Shop ..... 504 S. McDowell St.
Joe's Auto Repair Service ..... 2810 Statesville Ave.
Johnson's Barber Shop ..... 318 Cedar St. So.
Mack's Paint & Body Shop ..... 1422 Statesville Ave.
Maxie's Coffee House ..... 1425 Oaklawn Ave.
McDowell's Barber Shop ..... 502 McDowell St. So.
McGowan's Boarding House ..... 811 Oaklawn Ave.
Oaklawn Tavern ..... 1133 Oaklawn
Orr's Washeretta ..... 1100 Seaboard St.
Randolph's Grill ..... 806 S. Mint St.
Shu-Fixery ..... 425 W. 11 St.
The Griffith Street Luncheonette ..... Griffith St.
The Ideal Smoke Shop ..... 1122 Beatties Ford Rd.
The Igloo Dairy Bar ..... 1500 Beatties Ford Rd.
The Musical Grille ..... 802 S. McDowell St.
Third Ward Barber Shop ..... West Hill & Poplar St.
Welcome Grill ..... 207 N. McDowell St.
White Gable Cafe ..... 233 Frazier Ave.
White's Rendezvous ..... 2435 Lucene Ave.

DURHAM

Biltmora Hotel ..... 323 E. Pelligrew Street
Bull City Restaurant ..... 412 Pettigrew Street
College Inn Restaurant ..... 1306 Fayetteville
DeShazor's Hostelry ..... 809 Fayetteville Street

FAYETTEVILLE

Arthur's Sea Food Grill Restaurant ..... 637 Person
Coral Motor Court ..... U. S. 301, 3 mi. South
Jones Tourist Home ..... 311 Moore Street

King Cole Motel .... 2418 Murchison Rd.
Silver Grill Restaurant .... 115 Gillespie Street

GREENSBORO

Plaza Manor Hotel .... 511 Martin Street
T. Daniels Tourist Home .... 922 E. Market Street

GREENVILLE

Bell's Restaurant .... 604 Albemarle Avenue

HENDERSON

Adams Tourist Home .... 526 Chestnut Street

HIGH POINT

KILBY HOTEL .... **627 E. Washington Street**
Comfort, Convenience and Cleanliness

KINGS MOUNTAIN

Mrs. L. E. Ricks Tourist Home

KINSTON

Mark's Tourist Home & Cabins .... 105 W. South St.

NEW BERN

H. C. Sparrow Tourist Home .... 731 West St.
Rhone Hotel .... 512 Queen St.

RALEIGH

Bloodsworth St. Tourist Home .... 425 So. Bloodsworth St.
Deluxe Hotel .... 220 E. Cabarrus St.
Home Eckers Hotel .... 122 E. Hargett St.
Legion Home Restaurant .... 416 E. Cabarrus St.
New York Restaurant .... 108 E. Hargett St.
Stanton's Cafe-Restaurant .... 319 South East St.
Starksville Guest House .... 809 E. Bragg Street
Y.M.C.A. .... 600 So. Bloodworth St.

ROCKY MOUNT

Wright's Motel .... P. O. Box 43
Lincoln Park Motel .... 1000 Leggett Rd.

STATESVILLE

CARSON'S SERVICE STATION .... **636 S. Center Street**
Stop in for the best in general auto service.

Evening Breeze Motel .... On Hiway 70
FRANK'S GRILL .... 640 S. Center Street
Best of Foods — Phone 873-9250

STOKESDALE

Phone: Midway 3-3530 Open Year Round

JOHNSON'S SERVICE STATION & GROCERY

On Highway 158 Paul Johnson, Prop.

1½ Miles West of Stokesdale, N. C.
20 Miles East of Winston Salem, N. C.

WELDON

Pope Hotel
Terminal Inn Hotel .... Washington Avenue

WHITEVILLE

Mrs. Fannie Jeffers Tourist Home .... Mill Street

WILMINGTON

Johnson's Restaurant .... 1007 Chestnut Street
Owens Club 900 Restaurant .... 900 No. 9th Street
Paynes' Tourist Home .... 417 No. 6th Street

WINSTON SALEM

Charles H. Jones Tourist Home .... 1611 E. 14th Street

NORTH DAKOTA

Hotels — Motels — Tourist Homes — Restaurants

BISMARK

Grand Pacific Hotel
Motel Court .... Box 724

FARGO

Home Sweet Home Motel .... Hwys. 10 & 52

MINOT

Le Grand-Parker Hotel

MEDORA

Rough Riders Motel

WILLISTON

Clack Court Motel .... 2nd St., West at 11th St.

OHIO

Hotels — Motels — Tourist Homes — Restaurants

AKRON

Green Turtle Hotel .... Federal & Howard Street
Matthews Hotel .... 77 N. Howard Street

CINCINNATI

Club Tavern Hotel .... 2017 Seymour
Jim Williams Sohio Service Station .... 552 W. 9th Street
Lincoln Hotel .... 3166 Madison Road
Manse Hotel .... 1004 Chapel Street
O. Steele Tourist Home .... 3065 Kerper Street
Sinton .... Walter Latscha, Mgr. 4th & Vine
Y.W.C.A. .... 821 Lincoln Park Drive

CLEVELAND

Carnegie Hotel .... 6803 Carnegie Avenue
Majestic Hotel .... 2291 E. 55th Street

Manhattan Restaurant .... 9903 Cedar Avenue
Mrs. Edith Wilkins Tourist Home .... 2121 E. 46th Street
Mrs. Fannie Gilmer Tourist Home .... 12421 Benham Street

State Restaurant .... 7817 Cedar Avenue
Ward Hotel .... 4113 Cedar Avenue
Y.M.C.A. .... E. 76th & Cedar

COLUMBUS

Atcheson Restaurant .... 1288 Atcheson Street
B. & B. Restaurant .... 2015 Persons Avenue
Belmont Restaurant .... 1105 Oak Street
Bruce Latham Restaurant .... 317 Hosacks Street
Cooper Tourist Home .... 259 N. 17th Street
Deshler-Wallick Hotel .... Board & High Sts.
Duck Inn Restaurant .... 883 No. 4th Street
Hawkins Hotel .... 65 N. Monroe Avenue
Litchford Hotel .... North 4th Street
Macon Hotel .... 366 N. 20th Street
Neil House Hotel .... 35 South High Street
Newford Hotel .... 452½ E. Long Street
St. Clair Hotel .... 338 Ct. Clair Avenue
Turner's Restaurant .... 452½ E. Long Street

DAYTON

Cox's Cut Rate Drugs & Gifts .... 842 W. 5th Streeet
Vina's Luncheonette & Delicatessen .... 837 W. 5th Street
Whitey's Garage .... 512 S. Broadway
Y.M.C.A. .... 907 W. 5th Street

LIMA

George Cook Tourist Home .... 230 S. Union Street
Mrs. A. Turner Tourist Home .... 1215 W. Spring Street
Turner Hotel .... 1215 West Spring Street

LONDON

Mrs. James Pettress Tourist Home .... 26 E. Lincoln Avenue

LORAIN

H. P. Jackson Tourist Home .... 2383 Apple Avenue
Mrs. Alex Cooley Tourist Homes .... 114 W. 26th Street
Porter Wood Tourist Home .... 1759 Broadway
Worthington Tourist Home .... 209 W. 16th Street

PLAIN CITY

Madry's Travel Inn .... U. S. Hwy. 33, 20 mi. N.W., Columbus

PORT CLINTON

Woodlawn Cabins .... Rts. 2 & 163, 1/2 mile E. of Port Clinton

SANDUSKY

Hunter Hotel .... 407 W. Market Street

SPRINGFIELD

Mrs. M. E. Wilborn Tourist Home .... 220 Fair Street

Posey Hotel .... 209 S. Fountain Avenue

Posey Restaurant .... 211 S. Fountain Avenue

Y.M.C.A. .... Center Street

TOLEDO

COOK'S TOURIST HOME .... **1736-38 Washington Street**

Collingwood Motel .... Collingwood & Indiana Avenue

J. F. Watson Tourist Home .... 399 Pinewood Avenue

Mrs. J. Jennings Tourist Home .... 729 Indiana Avenue

YOUNGSTOWN

★HOTEL ALLISON .... **212 North West Avenue**

Fine Foods - Room Service - Free Parking — Tel. RI 6-9057

Belmont Tourist Home .... 327 Belmont Avenue

Central Restaurant .... 137 S. Center Street

Gold Inn Hotel .... 851 W. Federal Street

McDonald Hotel .... 442 E. Federal Street

Red Lion Motel .... 2019 Hubbard-Coitsville Rd.

Royal Palms Hotel .... 625 Hemrod Street

Y.M.C.A. .... 962 W. Federal Street

"Y" Restaurant .... 962 Federal Street

Blue Haven Cafe .... 371 E. Federal

Wee Motel .... 2705 McGuffey Rd.

ZANESVILLE

L. E. Costom Tourist Home .... 1545 W. Main Street

Little Harlem Restaurant .... Lee Street

OKLAHOMA

Hotels — Motels — Tourist Homes — Restaurants

ENID

Mrs. Johnson Tourist Home .... 217 E. Market Street

MUSKOGEE

Elliots Hotel .... 111 1/2 So. 2nd Street

People's Hotel .... 316 N. 2nd Street

OKLAHOMA CITY

Canton Hotel .... 200 N.E. 2nd Street

Hall Hotel .... 308 1/2 N. Central

Hotel Youngblood .... 4th & Stiles Sts.

Mrs. Lessie Bennett Tourist Home .... 500 N.E. 4th Street

Tucker's Tourist Home .... 315 1/2 N.E. 2nd Street

Wayside Motel .... 2028 N. Bryan Street

Y.M.C.A. .... 614 N.E. 4th Street

SHAWNEE

Olison Hotel .... 702 S. Bell

Slugg's Hotel .... 118 East Bently

SAPULA

Brooklyn Hotel .... 511 E. Hobson Street

SEMINOLE

Due Drop Inn .... 110 W. Wewaha Street

TULSA

Avalon Motel .... 2411 East Apache Street
C. U. Netherland Tourist Home .... 542 N. Elgin Street
Del Rio Hotel .... 607½ N. Greenwood
McHunt Hotel .... 1121 N. Greenwood Street
Miller Hotel .... 124 N. Hartford Street
Small Hotel .... 615 E. Archer
W. H. Smith Tourist Home .... 124½ N. Greenwood
Y.W.C.A. .... 1120 East Pine

OREGON

Hotels — Motels — Tourist Homes — Restaurants

ASTORIA

Astoria Court Motel .... 55 Olney Avenue

BEND

Cascade Court .... 846 South 3rd Street

CRATER LAKE

Crater Lake Lodge

EUGENE

City Center Lodge .... 476 E .Broadway

KLAMATH FALLS

Crater Cottages .... 2045 Oregon Avenue

PENDLETON

Pendleton Hotel

PORTLAND

Capitol Hill Motel .... 9110 S.W. Barbur Blvd.
Hotel Multnomah .... 319 S. W. Pine

SALEM

Salem Hotel .... Box 230

WALDPORT

Sea Stones Cottage .... 5 miles South on Hiway 101

PENNSYLVANIA

Hotels — Motels — Tourist Homes — Restaurants

ALLENTOWN

Southern Restaurant .... 372 Union Street

BEDFORD SPRINGS

Harris Hotel .... Penn. & West Sts.

CARLISLE

Lincoln Motel .... Box 114

CHESTER

Harlem Hotel .... 1909 W. 3rd Street
Vesta Vesta .... 311 Farnall Street

COATESVILLE

DeLoach Motor Lounge .... 420 Harry Rd.
Hotel Subway .... Coatesville

CRESCO

Mrs. Daniel L. Taylor Tourist Home

EAST STROUDSBURG

Fern Boarding House .... 387 Lincoln
Hillside Inn .... R.F.D. No. - (Hwy. 209)

ERIE

KINTUCKY BAR-B-QUE .... 1438 Parade Street
Visit us for the best ribs in town!
Pope Hotel .... 1318 French Street
WILSON'S SINCLAIR SERVICE STATION .... 17th & French Streets
General Repairs and Tune-ups — Service calls
Stake's House & Bar .... 1435 Parade Street

GERMANTOWN

Y.M.C.A. .... 132 W. Rittenhouse

HARRISBURG

Jack's Hotel .... 1002 North 6th Street
Mrs. W. D. Jones Tourist Home .... 1531 North 6th Street
Palace Hotel .... 1602 North 7th Street
Wishing Well Motel .... Hwy. 22, E. of Harrisburg

NEW CASTLE

Y.W.C.A. .... 312 N. Jefferson

OIL CITY

Mrs. Jackson Tourist Home .... 258 Bissel Avenue

HENRYVILLE

Lang's Orchard Cottage

MT. POCONO

Alenia's Inn — Anchor Inn

PHILADELPHIA

Bea's Hotel & Dining Room .... 1857 N. 17th Street
Bellevue-Stratford Hotel .... Broad & Walnut Sts.
Benjamin Franklin Hotel .... 9th & Chestnut Sts.
Brown's Restaurant .... N.E. Cor. 17th & Columbia Ave.
Burrell's Tourist Houses .... 306 N. 40th Street
Butler's Tavern .... S.W. Cor. 17th & Carpenter
Camp Mohawk .... 27 Upsal St.
Chesterfield Hotel .... Broad & Oxford Sts.
Essex House Hotel .... 13th & Filbert Sts.
Hoard's Southern Style Bar-B-Que .... 1841 Ridge Avenue
Hotel Linconia .... 1907 Fairmount Avenue
Horseshoe Hotel .... 12th & Lombard Sts.
Marriott Motor Hotel .... City Line & Monument Avenue
Tally's Paradise Hotel .... 1527 Fitzwater Street
Travelers Hotel .... 316 So. Broad Street
West End Hotel .... 420 N. 40th Street
Woodson Hotel .... 1330 Catherine Street

PITTSBURGH

B. Williams Tourist Home .... 1537 Howard Street
Birdie's Guest House .... 1522 Center Avenue
Elmore Hotel .... 2153 Webster Avenue
Flamingo Hotel .... 2407 Wylie Avenue
Hotel Webster Hall .... 4415—5th Avenue
Palace Hotel .... 1545 Wylie Avenue
Sherwyn Hotel
THE ELLIS HOTEL .... 2044 Center Avenue
Cocktail Bar & Lounge — Phone: 281-3269

POWELL
Winter's Farm

READING
Hotel Abraham Lincoln .... 100 North 5th Street
Mrs. C. Dawson .... 441 Buttonwood Avenue

SCRANTON
Hotel Scranton .... Vine & Wyoming

SELLERSVILLE
Mrs. Dorothy Scholls Tourist Home .... Forest Road

SWIFTWATER
Rose Tree Inn

WASHINGTON
Harley's Mapleview Motel .... U. S. Hwy. 19

WILKES BARRE

YORK
Mrs. I. Grayson Tourist Home .... 276 S. Belvidere Avenue
Yorktowne Hotel .... Market & Duke Sts.

RHODE ISLAND

Hotels — Motels — Tourist Homes — Restaurants

NEWPORT
Mrs. F. Jackson Tourist Home .... 28 Hall Avenue

PROVIDENCE
Hines Tourist Home .... 462 North Main Street

SOUTH CAROLINA

Hotels — Motels — Tourist Homes — Restaurants

AIKEN

C. F. Holland Tourist Home .... 602 Richland Avenue East

ANDERSON

Ess-Tee Restaurant .... 112 E. Church Street

Mrs. Sallie Galloway Tourist Home .... 420 Butler Street

BEAUFORT

DONALDSON'S FISHING .... Broad River
Camp & Lodge School Rd.

CHARLESTON

James Hotel .... 238 Spring Street

Mrs. Gladsen Tourist Home .... 15 Nassau Street

Mrs. Mayes Tourist Home .... 82½ Spring Street

CHERAW

College Inn Restaurant .... 324 2nd Street

Gate Grill .... Second Street

Mrs. Maggie Green .... 209 Church Street

Valerie Motor Inn .... 7 miles, south of Cheraw, S. C. on U. S. # 1

Live Oak Tourist .... 328 Second Street

COLUMBIA

Beachum Tourist Home .... 212 Gervais Street

College Inn Tourist Home .... 1609 Harden Street

Cozy Inn Restaurant .... 1509 Harden Street

Green Leaf Restaurant .... 1117 Wash. Street

Mom's Restaurant .... 1005 Washington Street

Mrs. H. Cornwell Tourist Home .... 1713 Wayne

Mrs. Irene B. Evans Tourist Home .... 1106 Pine Street

Mrs. J. P. Wakefield Tourist Home .... 816 Oak Street

Mrs. S. H. Smith Tourist Home .... 929 Pine Street

Mrs. W. D. Chappelle Tourist Home .... 1301 Pine Street

Nylon Hotel .... 918 Senate Street

Savoy Restaurant .... Old Winnsboro Street

Waverly Restaurant .... 2515 Gervais Street

Y.W.C.A. .... 230 Taylor Street

DARLINGTON

Mable's Motel .... Box 309

FLORENCE

Spring Valley Restaurant .... H'way 301

SOUTH DAKOTA

Hotels — Motels — Tourist Homes — Restaurants

ABERDEEN

Alonzo Ward Hotel .... S. Main Street
Virginia Restaurant .... 303 S. Main Street

BROOKINGS

Modern Wayside Motel .... 1430 6th Street

CUSTER

Rocket Court .... 211 Custer Ave. (U. S. 16 & 85)

PHILLIP

A. B. C. Motel .... U. S. 212

SIOUX FALLS

Mrs. J. Moxley Tourist Home .... 915 N. Main

WATERTOWN

5th Ave. & 212 Motel .... U. S. 212

TENNESSEE

Hotels — Motels — Tourist Homes — Restaurants

BRISTOL

MOROCCO MOTEL & GRILL .... 1200 Moore Street
Clean, Comfortable, Courteous Service.
Welcome to travelers.
Mrs. M. C. Brown Tourist Home .... 225 McDowell
Mrs. A. D. Henderson Tourist Home .... 320 Nelson St.

CHATTANOOGA

Dallas Hotel .... 230½ E. 9th Street
Kat's Korner Restaurant .... 601 Lincoln
La Grand Eat Shop .... 206 East 9th Street
M-Y-B Package Store .... 320 East 9th Street
Martin's Esso Center .... 3701 Alton Park Blvd.
Millender's Pharmacy .... 1800 East 3rd Street
Peoples Hotel .... 1104 Carter Street
Reuben's Place .... 411 East 9th Street

48 Rooms

AM 6-9979

Mrs. Ressie Harris,
Owner

QUINN'S HOTEL

The most fabulous Hotel for colored.

227 West Main at Cowart St.,

Chattanooga, Tenn.

4 Blocks from Downtown

on Highway 58, 11, 64, South

Ruby's Drive-In .... 101 E. 46th Street
Y.M.C.A. .... 915 Park Street
Y.W.C.A. .... 924 E. 8th Street

CLARKSVILLE

Northington Tourist Home .... 717 Main Street
Virginia's Cafe .... 908 E. College Street

CLEVELAND

Kline Rest Home .... 680 E. Inman Street, East
Quality Cafe .... 795 Inman Street

COLUMBIA

Stop & Rest Motel & Restaurant .... 4 mi. South on Hiway 31

HUMBOLDT

Booker T. Motel .... U. S. 79 & 70A

KNOXVILLE

Anderson's Tourist Home .... 501 E. Church Street
College Cafe .... 1518 University Ave., N.W.
Graves Drug Store .... 1901 Texas Avenue
Miller's Modern Motel & Resort .... On Hiway 11-W, 7 mi. East of Knoxville
Rosebud Tavern & Restaurant .... 120 E. Vine Avenue
Streamline Snack Bar .... 125 E. Vine Street
The Pink House .... 1514 University Ave., N.W.
Tommy's Service Station .... 1304 Vine Ave., S.E.

Toussaint L'Ouverture Post No. 80, American Legion .... 112 Main Ave., S.E.
Y.M.C.A. Cansler Branch .... 716 E. Church Avenue
Y.W.C.A. .... 2026 McCalla Avenue

MEMPHIS

Annie's Cafe .... 155 Beale Street
Cain Bros. Gulf Service & Garage .... 1252 Breedlove Street
Carnes Ave. Gulf Service Station & Garage .... 2585 Carnes Avenue
Eosary Hotel .... 181 Beale Avenue
Four Way Grill .... 998 Mississippi Blvd.
Georgia's Cafe .... 671 Mississippi Avenue
Handy House .... 995½ Mississippi Blvd.
Hotel Queen Ann .... 228 Vance Avenue
J. A. Ewing Service Station .... Mississippi & Alston Avenues
Jiffy Sundry .... 2509 Park Ave.
Lorraine Motel & Hotel .... 406 Mulberry Street
Marquette Hotel .... 507 Linden Street
Mitchells Hotel .... 160 Hernando Street
Mrs. Young's Tourist Home .... 1191 Smith Street
Nu-Way Service Station & Garage .... 855 Porter Street
Presley Gulf Station .... 181 W. Brooks Road
Ragland's Mobilgas Service Station .... 282 Beale Street
Sue's Bakery & Snack Bar .... 2902 Bradley Street
The Ann's Grill .... 186 E. Calhoun
The Cosmos Cafe .... 3514 Boxtown Road
The Friendly Three Cafe .... 416 Peoples Road
Travelers Hotel .... 347 Vance Avenue
United Taxi .... 240 Linden Avenue
Walker's Shell Service Station & Garage .... Bellevue at Vollintine
Ware's Super Market .... 226 W. Brooks Road
Ware's Texaco Station .... 337 W. Mitchell Road
Washburn's Mobilgas Service Station .... 941 Mississippi Avenue
Wells Sundry & Cafe .... 516 N. 3rd Street
White Star Cleaners .... 225 S. 4th Street

MURFREESBORO

Benford's Amoco Service Station .... 429 Maney Avenue
Moore's Tourist Home .... State & University Streets

NASHVILLE

Cozy Corner Restaurant & Tavern .... 1137 Jefferson Street
Eldorado Mofel .... 2806 Buchanan Street
Family Service Grocery .... 1601 Jefferson
Jet Restaurant .... 1815 Jefferson — 1510 Charlotte Ave.
Price's Dinner Club & Tavern .... 3020 Centennial Blvd.
R & R Liquor Store .... 1043 Jefferson
White's Lunch Room .... 2116 Meharry Blvd.
Y.M.C.A. .... 4th & Charlotte Avenues Y.W.C.A. .... 1708 Pearl Street
Driver's Shell Station .... AL 5-9370

TEXAS

Hotels — Motels — Tourist Homes — Restaurants

ABILENE

Mrs. Guy E. Rogers Tourist Home .... 550 No. 8th Street

AMARILLO

Tennessee Hotel .... 206 Van Buren Street
Tom's Place Restaurant .... 322 W. Third Street
Watley Hotel .... 112 Van Buren Street

ATLANTA

Mrs. Lizzie Simon Tourist Home .... 308 N. Howe Street

AUSTIN

Mrs. J. W. Duncan Tourist Home .... 1214 E. 7th Street
Porter's Tourist Home .... 1315 E. 12th Street
Southern Restaurant .... 1010 East 11th Street

BEAUMONT

Hotel Theresa .... 875 Neches Street
Long's Bar-B-Q .... 539 Forsythe Street
Mrs. B. Rivers Tourist Home .... 730 Forsythe Street

CORPUS CHRISTIE

Horace Crecy's Tourist Home .... 1710 Lexington Avenue
Avalon Restaurant .... 1510 Ramirez

DALLAS

Beaumont Barbeque Restaurant .... 1815 N. Field
Bogel Hotel .... 821 Bogel Street
Green Acres Motel .... 1711 McCoy Street
Howard Hotel .... 3118 San Jacinto Street
Powell Hotel .... 3115 State Street
Shalimar Restaurant .... 2219 Hall Street
Y.M.C.A. .... 2700 Flora Street
Y.W.C.A. .... 3525 State Street

DEL VALLE

Mayco Motel .... F. M. Rd. 973, Hwy. 71

EL PASO

C. Williams Tourist Home .... 1505 Wyoming Street
Daniel Hotel .... 413 S. Oregon Street
La Luz Motel .... 8064 Alameda (U. S. 80, East)
Mrs. S. W. Stull Tourist House .... 511 Tornillo

FORT WORTH

Clover Hotel .... 1901 East 4th Street
Evan's Tourist Home .... 1213 E. Terrell Street
Green Leaf Restaurant .... 315 E. 9th Street
Hotel Jim .... 413-15 E. Fifth Street
Monterey Hotel .... 1055 Evans Avenue
Y.M.C.A. .... 1604 Jones Street

GALVESTON

Gus Allen Hotel .... 2710 Ave. F
Little Shamrock Motel .... 1207 31st Street
Mrs. J. Pope Tourist Home .... 2824 M ½ Ave
Oleander Hotel .... 421½ 25th Street

HENDERSON

Chat & Chew Restaurant .... 615 N. Mill Street

HOUSTON

Ajapa Hotel .... 2412 Dowling Street
Crystal Hotel .... 3308 Lyons Avenue
Kirk Courts .... 2121 Kirk Street
La Jayo Hotel .... 4024 Lyons Avenue
Lincoln Restaurant .... Conti & Jenson
Mingo Motel .... 4749 Reed Road
New Day Hotel .... 1912 Dowling Street
Oriental Restaurant .... 2751 Lyons Avenue
Robinson's Manor .... 3211 Jackson Street
Sid's Ranch .... 8051 W. Montgomery

LONGVIEW

Eastman Road Motel .... Route 1, on Eastman Road

MARSHALL

Adkins West End Texaco Service Station .... 310 N. Bishop
Bailey Tourist Home .... 1103 W. Grand Avenue
La Casa Motel .... U. S. 80, 2 miles from Marshall
New Deal Ser. Station .... 618 S. Carter
Tucker's Gulf Service Station .... 900 Wiley

MEXIA

Mrs. M. Carroll Restaurant .... 109 N. Belknap Street

PORT ARTHUR

Ritz Hotel .... 708 Texas Avenue
Shadowland Restaurant .... 632 W. 7th Street
Tick Tock Restaurant .... 536 W. 7th Street

SAN ANTONIO

Mamie's Restaurant .... 1833 E. Houston Street
Manhattan Hotel .... 735 E. Commerce
Nolan Hotel .... 525 Nolan Street
Ritz Motel .... 2958 Commerce Street
Ross Hotel .... 126 N. Mesquite Street
Silver Slipper Restaurant .... 506 S. Gevers

TEXARKANA

Casino Restaurant .... 504 W. 3rd St.
The Wheel Motel .... 2207 W. 18th St.
Moore's Hotel .... 807 W. 4th St.

TYLER

Franklin Service Station .... Palace at Morris
Hotel Alfreda .... 1009 W. Morris Street
Mrs. Thomas Tourist Home .... 516 N. Border Street
North Palace Gulf Service Station .... 903 W. Lincoln
The Downbeat Cafe .... 906 Barret
W. Langston Tourist Home .... 1010 N. Border Street
White Sandwich Shop .... 420 N. Border Street
Wickware's Cities Service Station .... 628 N. Bois DArc

VAN HORN

McVay Courts .... Hwys. 80 - 90 & 54, 120 mi E. of El Paso

VICTORIA

Hotel Hayes .... 707 E. Stayton

WACO

B. Ashford Tourist Home .... 902 N. 8th Street
College View Motel .... East Elm Street

Ebony Motel .... 4723 Sanger
Ideal Restaurant .... 902 N. 8th Street

WAXAHACHIE

Mrs. M. Johnson Tourist Home .... 427 E. Main Street
Mrs. N. Lowe Tourist Home .... 418 E. Main Street

WICHITA FALLS

Bridges Hotel .... 404 Sullivan Street
E. B. Jeffrey Tourist Home .... 509 Juarez Street
Johnson's Restaurant .... 803 Harding Street
Mrs. L. Winson Tourist Home .... 607 Juarez Street
Plaza Hotel .... 423 Flood Street

UTAH

Hotels — Motels — Tourist Homes — Restaurants

BRYCE CANYON NATIONAL PARK

Bryce Canyon Inn .... Opens May 15th to Oct. 15th
Bryce Canyon Lodge .... Opens June 15th to Sept. 15th

CEDAR CITY

Cedar Crest Lodge Motel .... 555 So. Main Street

OGDEN

Royal Hotel .... 2522 Wall Avenue

PROVO

El Rancho Provo .... 1015 So. State

SALT LAKE CITY

Harlem Hotel .... 528½ West 2nd Street
Jenkins Hotel .... 250 W. South Temple
Sam Sneed Hotel .... 250 W. South Temple
St. Louis Hotel .... 242½ West South Temple
Y.W.C.A. .... 306 E. 3rd Street

ZION NATIONAL PARK

Zion Lodge .... Opens June 15th to Sept 15th
Zion Inn .... Opens May 15th to Oct. 15

VERMONT

Hotels — Motels — Tourist Homes — Restaurants

BURLINGTON

The Pates Hotel .... 86-90 Archiband Street

NORTHFIELD

Cole's Tourist Home .... 7 Sherman Avenue

RUTLAND

Meade Cottage Tourist Home .... 24 High Street

VIRGINIA

Hotels — Motels — Tourist Homes — Restaurants

AMHERST

Sam & Sarah Hudson Tourist Home .... Rte. 2, Box 256
Southern Style Bar-B-Que .... Norfolk Ave.
For Reservation Call 946-8721

BUCKROE BEACH

Bay Shore Hotel .... Buckroe Beach

CHARLOTTESVILLE

Carver Inn Hotel .... 701 Preston Avenue
Chauffeur's Rest Tourist Home .... 129 Preston Avenue
Alexander's Tourist Home .... 413 Dyce Street

CHASE CITY

RED DOOR RESTAURANT .... 8 East 5 Street
For the best flavor fo good food, give us a visit
THE GREEN DOOR RESTAURANT .... 12 West 5th Street
Unsurpassed for quality food and courteous service!

CHESTER

Colbrook Inn .... Rt. 3, Box 207

CHRISTIANBURG

Eureka Hotel

COVINGTON

Mrs. Loretta S. Watson Tourist Home .... 219 Lexington Street

DANVILLE

Mrs. M. K. Page Tourist Home .... 434 Holbrook Street
Mrs. Mary L. Wilson Tourist Home .... 401 Holbrook
Mrs. S. A. Overby Tourist Home .... Holbrok Street
Yancey's Tourist Home .... 320 Holbrook Street

DISPUTANTA

Forest View Motel .... 460 Norfolk Hwy.

DOSWELL

Hill Top Restaurant & Cabins .... Highway #1

EMPORIA

ATLANTIC ESSO STATION .... 107 E. Atlantic Street
C. A. Harris, Prop. — Phone: ME 4-2077

GLOUCESTER

Watkins Motel .... Gloucester

HAMPTON

Harriet's Drive-In .... 130 W. Pembroke Ave.
Kellam's Motel .... 185 Atlantic Ave.

JAMAICA

Oliver's Motel .... Highway 17 at Center Cross, Va.

LANEXA

R. & D. Motel .... Rte. 60

PHOEBUS-HAMPTON

The Rendezvous Cafe .... 58 Fulton St.

LAWRENCEVILLE

CORNER INN .... 409 N. Main Street
Beverly Taylor, Mgr.

LEXINGTON

Rose Inn .... 331 No. Main Street
The Franklin Tourist Home .... 9 Tucker Street

LURAY

Camp Lewis Mountain Tourist Home .... Skyline Drive
HOLLOWAY INN .... **RFD 2**
Special Attention to Families, Travelers, Hunters

LYNCHBURG

Happyland Lake Tourist Home .... 812 5th Avenue
Mrs. C. Harper Tourist Home .... 1109 8th Avenue
Mrs. N. P. Washington Tourist Home .... 611 Polk
Phyllis Wheatley Y.W.C.A. .... 613 Monroe St.

NEW KENT

Road Side Inn .... New Kent, Va.

NEWPORT NEWS

Al Smith's Service Station .... 2701 Marshall Ave.
Bob & Sam's Drive Inn .... 2811 Jefferson Ave.
Cosmos Hotel .... 620 25th St.
Grant's Restaurant .... 2108 Jefferson Ave.
Huggins Bar-B-Que .... 631 25th St.
Johnson's Room & Board .... 553 23rd St.
Clean, Comfortable Rooms — Phone' CH 7-5656
New York Barber Shop .... 2002 Jefferson Ave.
Norman's Service Station .... Hampton — Jefferson Ave.
Palm Tea Room .... 2146 Jefferson Ave.
Plaza Drive Inn .... 13537 Warwick Boulevard

NORFOLK

Foodarama .... 577 Church St.
★**PLAZA HOTEL .... 1757 Church St.**
Morning Glory Funeral Home .... 600 Chapel St.
Russell's Restaurant & Grill .... 816 Church St.
Regent Drive-In .... Shell Rd. & Delaware Ave.

PETERSBURG

Atlantic Cafe .... 103 Halifax St.
Colbrook Motel .... U. S. Rte. 1 & 301

PHOEBUS

Horton's Hotel .... County & Mellon Streets
Horton's Restaurant .... County & Mellon Streets

PORTSMOUTH

Benjamin's Confectionery & Dining Room .... 223 S. Green St.
Beuie's Esso Service Station .... 1701 Effingham St.
Blue Haven Hotel .... 401 S. Green St.
Combo Terrace .... On Hiway #13 and 460
Sportsman's Restaurant & Motel .... On Rte. 2 nr. Portsmouth
Fagan's Seaford Restaurant .... Cor. Gosport Rd. & Pine St.
Holmes Bros. Sinclair Service Station .... 3415 Gosport Rd.
Jimmie's Flying A Service Station .... 1201 Langley Blvd.
Kelly's Restaurant & Motel .... 801 County St.
Marshall's Cities Service Station .... 1808 Gosport Rd.
Ransdell's Motel .... 630 London St.

RICHMOND

Eggleston Hotel .... 2nd & Leigh
Harris Hotel .... 200 E. Clay Street
Slaughter Hotel .... 529 N. 2nd Street
Y.WC.A. .... Orange Avenue
Perry's Restaurant .... 519 N. 2nd St.
Skinney's Bar-B-Que .... Fairmount Ave. at 25th St.
Otto's Inn .... 314 No. 2nd St.

ROANOKE

Colvin's Tourist Home .... 16 Kilmer Avenue, N. W.

Dumas Hotel .... Henry Street, N. W.
Y.W.C. .... 416 Gainbore Rd., N. W.
Colvin's Tourist Home .... 16 Gilmer Avenue, N. W.
Brooks Pharmacy .... 221 N. Henry Street

SOUTH HILL

Brown's New Cafe .... 105 E. Virginia St.

STAUNTON

Pannell's In, Tourist Home .... 613 N. Augusta Street

STORMONT

Midway Auto Repair .... Urbanna Road
G. L. Davis Service Station .... Cook's Corner

SUFFOLK

E & L Lassiter Pur Oil Station .... 802 E. Washington St.
Nansemond Co-Op Servicenter .... 133 Tyne sStreet
Suffolk Professional Pharmacy, Inc. .... 362 E. Washington St.

TAPPAHANNOCK

Mark Haven Beach Hotel .... Tel.: Hillcrest 3-3871
McGuire's Inn Hotel .... Marsh Street

WEST POINT

Jordan's Enterprises .... 14th & Kirby Streets
Morton's Restaurant .... 221 15th Street

WILLIAMSBURG

Grove's Esso Service Center .... Route 2 - Box 228

WINCHESTER

Ruth's Restaurant .... 128 E. Cecil Street

WASHINGTON

Hotels — Motels — Tourist Homes — Restaurants

BELLINGHAM

Bell's Auto Court .... 208 Samish Highway
Leopold Hotel .... 1224 Cornwall Ave.

BREMERTON

Enetai Hotel .... 318 Washington Ave.

GRAND COULEE

Continental Hotel

OLYMPIA

Hotel Olympian

RANIER NATIONAL PARK

Paradise Inn
Paradise Lodge

SEATTLE

Atlas Hotel .... 420 Maynard Street
Eagle Hotel .... 408½ Main Street
Benjamin Franklin .... 5th Ave. & Virginia
Commodore Hotel .... 2013 2nd Ave.
Doric Mayflower .... 4th & Olive Way
Doric New Washington .... 2nd & Stewart St.
Edmond Meany Tourist Home .... 45th & Brooklyn East
Green Hotel .... 711 Lane Street
Mar Hotel .... 511 Maynard Avenue
New Richmond Hotel .... 308 4th Avenue
Olympus Hotel .... 413 Maynard Street
Welcome Annex Hotel .... 613½ Jackson Avenue

TACOMA

Dittemore's Court .... 12701 Pacific Highway
Monte Carlo Hotel .... 1555 Tacoma Avenue
Travelers Restaurant .... 1506½ Pacific Avenue
Winthrop Western Hotel .... 9th and Broadway

VANCOUVER

Ricketon's New Motel .... 4010 Main Street

YAKIMA

Senator Hotel

WEST VIRGINIA

Hotels — Motels — Tourist Homes — Restaurants

BECKLEY

New Pioneer Hotel .... 340 S. Fayette Street

BLUEFIELD

Travelers' Inn Hotel .... 1039 Wayne Street

CHARLESTON

Ferguson's Hotel .... Washington Street
Penn's Hotel .... West Charleston

CLARKESBURG

Mrs. Ruby Thomas Lodgings .... 126 Maud St.

FRANKLIN

Hotel Franklin .... 129½ Main Street

GRAFTON

Jones' Restaurant .... Latrobe Street

HINTON

Maya's Guest House .... State Street
The Price House Hotel .... 109 2nd Avenue

HUNTINGTON

Mrs. C. J. Barnett Lodgings .... 810 7th Avenue
Spot Restaurant .... 1614 8th Avenue
The Ross House Hotel .... 911 8th Avenue

MONTGOMERY

New Royal Hotel .... 223 Gaines Street

MORGANTOWN

Mrs. Jeannette O. Parker Lodgings .... 2 Cayton
Mrs. Linnie Mae Slaughter Lodgings .... 3 Cayton

MOUNDSXILLE

Mrs. Blanche Campbell Lodgings .... 1206 4th Street

NORTHFORK

Houchins Hotel & Cafe

WELCH

Capehart Hotel .... 14 Virginia Avenue

WHITE SULPHUR SPRINGS

Slaughter's Tourist Home

WISCONSIN

Hotels — Motels — Tourist Homes — Restaurants

ASHLAND

Stone's Motel .... RFD #3

BELOIT

Beloit Hotel
Hobson Motel .... 102-110 Park Avenue

ELM GROVE

Sleepy Hollow Motel .... 12600 W. Blue Mound Rd.

GREEN BAY

Beaumont Hotel .... Box 643

LA CROSSE

Linker Hotel

Nuttleman's Lodge Motel .... Hwy. 16

MILWAUKEE

Ambassador Motel Hotel .... 2308 W. Wisconsin Ave.

Astor .... 924 E. Juneau Ave.

Milwaukee Inn .... E. State St. & Lake

Schroeder .... 509 W. Wisconsin Ave.

Shorecrest .... 1962 N. Prospect Ave.

Carl's Restaurant .... 628 W. Juneau Avenue

Chicken Shack Restaurant .... 537 W. Walnut Street

Hillcrest Hotel .... 504 W. Galena Street

Mrs. M. Burns, Rooming House .... 1241 N. 6th Street

Pastell Lampkins Roming House .... 2427 N. 14th Street

Y.W.C.A. .... 915 W. Wisconsin Avenue

OSHKOSH

Hotel Raulf .... 530 N. Main St.

RACINE

Hotel Racine .... 535 Main St.

SUPÈRIOR

Hotel Saratoga

WISCONSIN DELLS

Lazy "M" Dude Ranch .... Route 2, River Road

WYOMING

Hotels — Motels — Tourist Homes — Restaurants

CASPER

Blue Spruce Motel .... 1914 Yellowstone, East

CHEYENNE

★MINNEHAHA MOTEL .... **1905 E. Lincolnway**

ROCK SPRINGS

Collins Tourist Home .... 915 7th Avenue

Liberty Motel .... U. S. 30

YELLOWSTONE NATIONAL PARK

Grand Canyon

Mammoth Hot Springs Hotel

Old Faithful Inn

BERMUDA

HAMILTON

Blue Jay Restaurant .... Church Street

Imperial Hotel .... Church Street

Ripleigh Guest House .... Mrs. Doris Pearman

The Spot Restaurant .... Burnaby Street

PEMBROKE

Milestone Guest House .... Coxs Hill

Richmond House Hotel .... Richmond Road

ST. GEORGE'S

"Archlyn Villa," Guest House....Wellington Street
St. George's Hotel

TUCKER'S TOWN

Castle Harbor Hotel

WARRICK

Hilton Manor Guest House....Mrs. W. Tucker, Prop.
Homeleigh Guest House....Mrs. D. Eave, Prop.
Mrs. Leon Eve Guest House....Snake Road

W. PEMBROKE

Sunset Lodge Guest House....P. O. Box 413

CONVENTION AND CONFERENCE CALENDAR

May 3- 5 National Epicureans, Inc., Washington, D. C. (Presidential Arms)
May 17-19 The Moles, Inc., Washington, D. C.
May 24-25 Girl Friends, Inc., Chicago, Ill.
May 29-31 National Alliance of Postal Employees, Miami, Fla. (Hampton House)
May 18 National Council of Negro Women, Inc., Washington, D. C. (Commemration meeting)
June 7- 9 Chi Delta Mu Fraternity, Washington, D. C. (Statler-Hilton)
June 25-28 National Association of Ministers' Wives, Atlanta, Ga. oration Meeting
June 25-30 Chi Eta Phi Sorority, Inc., Durham, N. C.
July 1- 7 National Association For the Advancement of Colored People, Chicago, Ill. (Morrison Hotel)
July 15-21 Bible Way Church of Our Lord Jesus Christ World Wide, Inc., Washington, D. C.
July 16-20 Zeta Phi Beta Sorority, Inc., Miami, Fla. (Miami Municipal Auditorium)
July 16-21 National Assn. of Fashion And Accessory Designers, Inc. Chicago, Ill. (Sheraton)
July 22-26 National United Church Ushers Assn. of America, Inc. Baltimore, Md.
July 25-27 Lambda Kappa Mu Sorority, Inc., Syracuse, N. Y.
July 28-Aug. 1 National Urban League, Los Angeles, Calif. (Statler-Hilton)
July 31-Aug 3 American Teachers Assn., Dallas, Tex.
Aug. 3- 9 Woman's Home & Foreign Missionary Society, AME Zion Church, St. Louis Mo. (Washington Metropolitan AMEZ Ch.)
Aug. 4- 8 National Beauty Culturists League, Inc., Chicago, Ill.
Aug. 4- 9 National Dental Assn., Inc., Philadelphia, Pa. (Sheraton)
Aug. 5- 9 National Convention of Gospel Choirs & Chouses, Inc. Pittsburgh, Pa.
Aug. 6-11 National Sorority of Phi Delta Kappa, Los Angeles, Calif.
Aug. 10-16 Iota Phi Lambda Sorority, Inc., Youngstown, Ohio
Aug. 11-15 National Funeral Directors & Morticians Assn., Columbus, O. (Deshler-Hilton)
Aug. 13-18 Tau Gamma Delta Sorority, New York, N. Y. (Waldorf Astoria)
Aug. 12-15 National Medical Assn., Los Angeles, Calif. (Statler Hilton)
Aug. 12-15 Women's Auxiliary to the National Medical Assn., Los Angeles, Calif.
Aug. 12-17 Sigma Gamma Rho Sorority, Inc., Denver, Colo. (Brown Palace)
Aug. 14-18 National Assn. of College Women, Chicago, Ill. (Morrison)
Aug. 16-22 Alpha Phi Alpha Fraternity, Inc., Boston, Mass. (Statler Hilton)
Aug. 17-24 National Supreme Council Ancient & Accepted Scottish Rite Masons, Miami, Fla. (Hampton House)
Aug, 17-24 National Grand Chapter Order of Eastern Star, Miami, Fla.

Aug. 18-21 Supreme Lodge Knights of Pythias, Hot Springs, Ark. (Pythian Hotel)
Aug. 18-23 Ancient Egyptian Arabic Order Nobles of the Mystic Shrine, Pittsburgh, Pa. (Penn-Sheraton)
Aug. 18-23 Imperial Court-Daughters of Isis, Pittsburgh, Pa. (Penn-Sheraton)
Aug. 18-23 National Assn. of Negro Musicians, Columbus, Ohio
Aug. 19-23 National Insurance Assn., Chicago, Ill. (Sheraton-Chicago)
Aug. 20-23 Frontiers International, Inc., Chicago, Ill. (Sheraton)
Aug. 25-29 National Assn. of Real Estate Brokers, Inc., Chicago, Ill. (Sherman House)
Aug. 26-30 Improved Benevolent Protective Order of Elks of the World, Boston, Mass.
Aug. 26-30 Grand Temple Daughters of I.B.P.O.E. of W. Boston, Mass
Aug. 28-Sept. 2 National Technical Assn., Chicago, Ill.
Sept. 3- 8 National Baptist Convention, U.S.A., Inc., Cleveland, Ohio
Oct. 13-16 National Hotel Assn., Inc., New Orleans, La. (Mason's Motel)
Dec. 26-30 Phi Beta Sigma Fraternity, Inc., Nashville, Tenn. (Tenn. A & I State U.)

Excerpts from "When They Meet" compiled by Joseph V. Baker Associates, Inc. for Hamlton Watch Company.

CANADA

Hotels — Motels — Tourist Homes — Restaurants

ONTARIO

BRANTFORD
Graham Bell Hotel...48 Dalhousie St.

CORNWALL
Lloyd George Hotel ....15 Pitt St.

FT. WILLIAM
Adanae Hotel ....227 Simpson St.

HAMILTON
Crestwood Hotel
4 miles east on #2 Hwy.
Fischer Hotel ....51 York St.
Sheraton-Connaught Hotel & Motor Inn..............112 King St., E.
Wentworth Arms Motor Hotel
Main & Hughson St.

LONDON
London Hotel
Dundas & Wellington St.

NIAGARA FALLS
Foxhead Motor Inn
Falls Ave. & Clifton Hill
Park Hotel ....Clifton Hill
Sheraton-Breck Hotel
1685 Falls Ave.

OTTAWA
Bytown Inn ....73 O'Connor St.
Chateau Laurier
Rideau St. (Hwy 17)
Lord Elgin ....Elgin & Laurier Ave.
Rock Haven Motel
597 Montreal Rd.

PORT ARTHUR
Port Arthur Motor Hotel
N. Cumberland St.

SAULT STE. MARIE
Sault Windsor Hotel
617 Queen St., E.

TORONTO
Anndore Hotel ......15 Charles St., .E
Constellation Hotel
Dixon Rd. & Renforth Dr.
Four Seasons Motor Hotel
Jarvis & Carlton St.
Frontenac Arms ....306 Jarvis St.
Glenview Terraces Hotel
2904 Yonge St.
King Edward Sheraton
37 King St., E.
Lido Motel......................West Hill P. O.
Lord Simcoe
University Ave. & King St.
Park Plaza ......Bloor St. & Avenue Rd.
Regency Towers ....89 Avenue Rd.
Royal York ....Front St.
Skyline Hotel ....655 Dixon Rd.

WINDSOR
Bali-Hi Motor Hotel
1280 Ouellette Ave.
Norton Palmer ....130 Park St., W.

MONTREAL

Berkeley Hotel ... 1188 Sherbrooke St., W.
Capri ... 6445 Decarie Blvd.
Cartier Motel ... 14070 Sherbrooke St. E.
De La Salle ... 1240 Drummond St.
Laurentien Hotel ... 1130 Windsor St.
New Carlton ... 915 Windsor St.
Queen Elizabeth ... 900 Dorchester St., W.
Queen's Hotel ... 700 Windsor St.
Ritz Carlton ... Sherbrooke St., W.
Sheraton-Mt. Royal ... 1455 Peel St.
Skyline Hotel ... 6050 Cote de Liesse Rd.

QUEBEC

Chateau Frontenac ... Place d'Armes
Chateau Laurier ... 695 Grand Allee
Manoir St. Castin ... P. O. Lae Beauport, Que.

MOOSE JAW

Harwood Hotel ... 30 Fairford St., E.

REGINA

King's Hotel ... 1746 Searth St.
Saskatchewan Hotel ... Victoria Ave. (Hwy 1)

SASKATEEN

Albany Hotel ... 20th St. & Ave. B
Bessborough ... Spadina Crescent & 21st
King George ... 157 Second Ave., N.
Senator ... 243 - 21st St., E.

MEXICO

ACAPULCO

Acapulco Hilton ... Avenida Miguel Aleman
Boca Chica ... Playa Caletilla
Caleta ... P.O. Box 76, Caleta Beach
Club De Pesea ... Costera Miguel Aleman 60
Del Monte ... Cerro de la Pinzina (P.O. Box 55)
El Morador ... La Quebrada
El Presidente ... Avenida Miguel Aleman
Las Brisas Hilton ... Escenica Hwy.

CUERNAVACA

Motor Hotel Mandel ... Blvd. & Zapata 801 (Hwy 95)

GUADALAJARA

California Courts ... Av. Vallarta 2525
Camino Real ... Calz. del Nino & Vallarta
Turiservicios, S. A. ... Vallarta 2785

GUAYMAS

Playa de Cortes ... Bahia de Bacochibampo (P.O. Box 66)

JUAREZ

Hotel Continental ... Lerdo 178
Hotel San Antonio ... Av. 16 de Septiembre 634
Hotel Sylvias ... Av. 16 de Septiembre 1587
Tourist Camp—Jardin Fronterizo ... American H'way #7
Hotel Moran ... Av. Juarez 238

MEXICAN GOVT. TOURIST BD.

MAZATLAN

Playa Mazatlan .... P. O. Box 207

MERIDA

Panamericana .... 59th St., No. 455

MEXICO CITY

Alameda .... Ave. Juarez 50
Ambassador .... Humboldt No. 38
Continental Hilton
Paseo de la Reforma 166
Cortes .... Ave. Hidalgo 85
Del Prado Hotel .... Av. Juarez 70
El Presidente .... Hamburgo 135
Francis
Paseo de la Reforma & Morelos
Geneve .... 130 Londres St.
Guardiola .... Madero 5
Luma .... Orizaba 16
Majestic .... Madero No. 73
Meurice .... Calle Marsella 28
Monte Cassino .... Genova 56
Prado-Aiffer .... Revillagijedo 18
Ritz .... Madero 30

MONTERREY

Ambassador
Hidalgo & Galeana St.
Anfa Super Motel
Hwy 85 N., Kilometer 995
Gran Hotel Aneira .... Plaza Hidalgo

MORELIA

Virrey de Mendoza
Portal Matameros 16

PATZCUARE

Posada De Don Vasco
Av. Americas Unidas

TAXCO

Loma Linda Motel
Hwy 95 at Kilometer 161
Posada De La Mision
Calle de la Mision 32

THE CARIBBEAN

Hotels — Motels — Tourist Homes — Restaurants

BARBADOS TOURIST BD.

ANTIGUA

Admirals Inn .... English Harbour
Anchorage .... Dickenson Bay
Antigua Beach .... Hodges Bay
Antigua Horizons .... Long Bay
Balgowne Guest House .... St. John's
Barrymore .... Fort Rd.
Beachcomber .... Coolidge
Blue Waters .... Soldier Bay
Caribbean Beach Club
Dickejsen Bay
Curtain Bluff .... Old Road
Galley Bay Surf Club .... Galley Bay
Half Moon Bay .... Half Moon Bay
Hawksbill .... Five Islands
Jolly Beach .... Jolly Hill Bay
Kensington House .... St. John's
Long Bay .... Long Bay
Lord Nelson Club .... Coolidge
Stephendale .... St. John's
Sugar Mill .... Coolidge
The Inn .... English Harbour
Trade Winds .... Dickenson Bay
White Sands .... Hodges Bay

ARUBA

Aruba Caribbean Hotel .... Casino

BARBADOS

Abbeville .... Christ Church
Accra Beach .... Christ Church

BARBADOS TOURIST BD.

Aquatic Club .... St. Michael
Bagshot House .... Christ Church
Blue Water .... Christ Church
Bonnie Dundee .... Christ Church
Bowden .... Christ Church
Cacrabank .... Christ Church
Caribbee .... Christ Church
Colony Club .... St. James
Coral Reef .... St. James
Crane .... St. Philip
Eastry House .... St. Peter
Edgewater .... St. Joseph
Island Inn .... St. Michael
Marine .... Christ Church
Miramar .... St. James
Ocean View .... Christ Church
Paradise Beach Club .... St. Michael
Powell Spring .... St. Joseph
Rockley Beach .... Christ Church
Royal Caribbean .... Christ Church
Royal-On-Sea .... Christ Church
St. Lawrence .... Christ Church
Sam Lord's .... St. Philip
Sandy Beach .... Christ Church
Sandy Lane .... St. James
San Remo .... Christ Church
Sea View .... Christ Church
Shoe String .... Christ Church
Stonehaven Inn .... St. Philip
South Winds .... Christ Church
Sunset Lodge .... St. Peter
Swiss Chalet .... St. James
White Sands .... Christ Church

BRITISH GUIANA

Park .... Georgetown
Tower .... Georgetown
Woodbine .... Georgetown

BRITISH HONDURAS

Bellevue .... Belize
Fort George .... Belize

DOMINICA

Cherry Lodge .... Roseau
Clarke Hall .... Layou
South Chiltern .... St. Paul
Springfield .... Imperial Rd.
Sutton .... Roseau

GRAND CAYMAN

Bay View .... Georgetown
Beach Club Colony
West Bay Beach
Buccaneer's Inn .... Cayman Brac
Coral Caymanian .... Georgetown
Emerald Beach Apts. .... South Sound
Galleon Beach .... Georgetown
Pageant Beach .... Georgetown
Rum Point .... Rum Point
Sea View .... Georgetown
Sunset House .... Georgetown

GRENADA

Antilles .... St. George's
Crescent Inn .... Belmont-Grand Anse
Elite Guest House .... St. George's
Green Gables .... St. George's
Grenada Beach .... Grand Anse
St. James .... St. George's
Silver Sands .... Grand Anse
Spice Island .... Grand Anse
The Islander .... St. George's

GUADELOUPE

Au Grand Corsaire .... Gosier

Dole-Les-Bains ....Gourbeyre
Grand ....Pointe-A-Pitre
Normandie ....Pointe-A-Pitre
Royal ....Basse-Terre
Vielle Tour ....Gosier

JAMAICA (Kingston Area)

Abahati ....Kingston
Abbey Court ....Kingston
Blue Mt. Inn ....Gordon Town
Courtleigh Manor ....Kingston
Flamingo ....Kingston
Green Gables ....Kingston
Kingsley ....Kingston
Liguanea Terrace ....Kingston
Manor House ....Kingston
Melrose ....Kingston
Mimosa ....Kingston
Mona ....Kingston
Morgan's Harbour ....Pt. Royal
Myrtle Bank ....Kingston
Sheraton Kingston ....Kingston
South Camp ....Kingston
Stony Hill ....Kingston
Strawberry Hill ....Irish Town
Terra Nova ....Kingston

(Mandeville Area)

Mandeville ....Mandeville
Mayflower ....Mandeville

(Montego Area)

Bay Roc ....Montego Bay
Beach View ....Montego Bay
Black Swan ....Montego Bay
Blairgowrie ....Montego Bay
Casa Blanca ....Montego Bay
Casa Montego ....Montego Bay
Chatham ....Montego Bay
Colony ....Montego Bay
Coral Cliff ....Montego Bay
Corniche Studio Apts. Montego Bay
Gloucester House ....Montego Bay
Good Hope Plantation ....Falmouth
Hacton House ....Montego Bay
Half Moon ....Montego Bay
Harmony House ....Montego Bay
Miranda Lodge ....Montego Bay
Montego Beach ....Montego Bay
Montego Inn ....Montego Bay
Montego Bay Racket Club
Montego Bay
Richmond Hill ....Montego Bay
Round Hill ....Montego Bay
Royal Caribbean ....Montego Bay
Silver Sands ....Duncans
Sunset Lodge ....Montego Bay
Tropical Terrace..................Montego Bay
Tryall ....Sandy Bay

(Ocho Rios & North Shore)

Arawak ....Ocho Rios
Carib-Ocho ....Ocho Rios
Casa Maria ....Port Maria
Eaton Hill ....Runaway Bay
Falcondip ....Ocho Rios
Golden Head Beach ....Oracabessa
Hibiscus Lodge ....Ocho Rios
Jamaica Inn ....Ocho Rios
Marrakesh Beach ....Ocho Rios
Plantation Inn ....Ocho Rios
Runaway Bay Hotel ....Runaway Bay
Sans Souci ....Ocho Rios
Shaw Park Beach Club ....Ocho Rios
Silver Seas ....Ocho Rios
Tower Isle ....Ocho Rios
Windsor ....St. Ann's Bay

(Port Antonio)

Domontevin Lodge ....Port Antonio

MARTINIQUE

Atlantique ....Lorrain
Auberge de L'Anse Mitan
Treis-liest
Auberge du Manoir
Route de Moutte
Auberge du Vieux Chalet
Morne-Rouge
Berkeley ....Fort-de-France
Bristol ....Fort-de-France
Gallia
Hotel Central et Europe
Hotel de France ....Mormo-Rouge
Imperatrice ....Fort-de-France
La Dunette ....Sainte-Anne
Les Pitons ....Balata
Lido ....Fort-de-France

PUERTO RICO

AGUADILLA

Montemar Hotel

ARECIBO

Mir Hotel

BARRANQUITAS

El Barranquitas Hotel

DORADO

Dorado Beach Hotel

PONCE

El Ponce Intercontinental

SAN JUAN

Americana of San Juan
P. O. Box 5628, Isla Verde

Atlantic Beach
Vendig St. (Santurce)

Bird El Hato Rey
452 Ponce de Leon Ave.

Caribe Hilton

Condado Beach .... Box 3552

Condado Lagoon
Jeffre & Clemenceau St.

El Miramar Charterhouse
Av. Olimpio 60

El San Juan .... P. O. Box 389

Escambron

International Airport
Airport Terminal Bldg.

Sheraton-San Juan

Normandie

Pierre

ST. KITTS

Blakeney .... Basseterre

Palms .... Basseterre

Royal

Seaside

The Cockleshells .... Salt Pond

ST. LUCIA

Blue Waters Beach .... Castries

James

St. Antoine

St. Lucia Beach .... Gres Islet

Villa .... Castries

ST. VINCENT

Blue Caribbean .... Kingstown

Blue Lagoon .... Rathe Mill

Hadden .... Kingstown

Heron

Olive's

Sugar Mill Inn .... Rathe Mill

Sunny Caribbee .... Bequia

Villa Lodge .... Villa

VIRGIN ISLANDS

ST. CROIX

Buccaneer Hotel
Club Comanche
Cottages By the Sea
The Cruzana
Estate Belvedere
Estate Good Hope
Grapetree Bay Hotel
Hotel-On The Cay
King Christian Hotel
Mahogany Inn
Pink Fancy Apts.
Sprat Hall
St. Croix Beach Hotel
Sunset Cottages
Turquoise Bay Cottages
Village At Cane Bay
The Waves

ST. JOHN

Caneel Bay Plantation
Gallows Point

ST. THOMAS

Adams Guest House
Bluebeard's Castle
Bluebeard's Beach Club
Caribbean Beach Hotel
Cromwell House
Domini Hus
Dorothea Beach Club
Enchanted Hill Guest House
Estate Contant
Flamboyant Hotel
Gramboko Inn
Harbor View
Holiday House
Holland House
Island Beachcomber
Kriss Guest House
La Borde's Guest House
Mafloie Apartment Hotel
Midtown Guest House
Miller Manor
Morning Star Beach Resort
Mountain Top
Nibbs-Ville
Sapphire Bay Beach Club
Sea Horse Inn
Smith's Fancy
Surfside
The Gate
Trade Winds Hotel
Tropic Isle Hotel
Vialet's Villa Guest House
Villa Santana
Virgin Island Hilton
Water Isle Hotel & Beach Club
Yacht Haven Cottage Resort

TOBAGO

Arnes Vale .... Plymouth

Bacolet .... Scarborough

Bird of Paradise .... Speyside
Bluehaven .... Scarborough
Castle Cove .... Scarborough
Crown Point .... Crown Point
Della Mira .... Scarborough
Robinson Crusoe .... Scarborough

TRINIDAD

Bel Air .... Piarco
Bergerac .... Port of Spain
Bretton Hall
Normandie
Pelican Inn
Piarco Guest House .... Piarco
Queen's Park .... Port of Spain
Simpson's Shoreland ... Point Cumana
Trinidad Hilton .... Port of Spain
Tropical .... Maraval

COSTA RICA

SAN JOSE

Europa Hotel
Central St. at 5th Ave.

SAN SALVADOR

El Salvador Intercontinental

GUATAMALA

GUATAMALA CITY

Guatamala-Biltmore
La Reforma y 15 Calle
Maya Excelsior ..... 7a Ave. No. 12-46

HONDURAS

TEGUEIGALPA, D. C.

Gran Hotel Lincoln

NICARAGUA

MANAGUA

Gran Hotel .... Av. Central N. 41

PANAMA

PANAMA CITY

Siesta Hotel .... nr. Locumen Airport
Panama Hilton .... via Estana
Hotel Continental .... via Estana
Hotel Internacional,
Plaza Cinco de Mayo

SOUTH AMERICA

ARGENTINA

BUENOS AIRES

City Hotel .... Bolivar 160
Claridge .... Tucuman 535
Continental
Av. Reque Saenz Pena 725
Plaza Hotel .... Florida y Charcas

BRAZIL

BRASILIA

Nacional-Brasilia ..... Seter Hoteleirc

CAMPINAS

Terminus
Avenida Francisco Glicerio 1075

RECIFE

Grande
Avenida Martins de Barros, 593
Guararapes .... Rua da Palma s/n

RIO DE JANEIRO

Excelsior Copacabana
Avenida Atlantica 1800
Ouro Verde
Avenida Atlantica, 1456 Copabana

BARBADOS TOURIST BD.

PANAMA TOURIST BD.

SALVADOR

Plaza de Salvador
Avenida Sete de Setembro, 212

SAO PAULO

Excelsior Hotel ....Ov. Ipiranga 770
Iaragua ....Rua Major Quedinho 40

CHILE

SANTIAGO

Carrera Hilton Hotel
Teatinos No. 180

COLOMBIA

BARRANQUILLA

Central Hotel ....Calle 38 #41-122

BOGOTA

Tequendama Hotel
Carrera 10, #26-21

PERU

LIMA

Gran Hotel Bolivar
Plaza San Martin
Savoy ....Caylloma 224

URUGUAY

MONTEVIDEO

Victoria Plaza
Plaza de la Independencia 759

VENEZUELA

CARACAS

Avila
El Conde
Macuto-Sheraton

EUROPE

AUSTRIA

Altausee ....House Eibl
Badgastein ....Mozart
Graz ....Hotel Daniel
Heiligenblut ....Alpenhotel Kaiser
Innsbruck ....Hotel Tyrol, Hotel Kreid
Obergurgl ....Hotel Haus Burger
Portschach ....Hotel Minerva
Salzburg ....Pension Eibl
Seeboden am Millstattersee ....Royal Hotel Seehof
Vienna ....Hotel Bristol, Hotel de France

BELGIUM

Antwerp ....Grand Hotel Londres, Queen's Hotel, Metropole Hotel
Bastogne ....Hotel Lebrun
Blankenberge ....Hotel Petit Rouge, Hotel Ideal
Bouillon ....Hotel De La Post, Hotel Du Panorama
Bruges ....Hotel Memlinc
Brussels ....Hotel Mayfair, Hotel Plaza, Hotel des Colonies
Charleroi ....Grand Hotel Siebertz
De Haan (Le Coq) ....Hotel Astoria
Ghent ....Hotel Cour St-Georges
Rochefort ....Grand Hotel du Centre
Spa ....Grand Hotel Britannique

DENMARK

Aalborg ....Hotel Phoenix
Copenhagen ....Hotel d'Angleterre, Grand Hotel, Hotel Excelsior
Fredensborg ....Hotel Frederik IV
Fredrikshavn ....Hoffmanns Hotel
Helsingor ....Hotel Marienlyst
Snekkersten ....Hotel Kystens Perle
Mon ....Hotel Store Klint

EIRE

Bantry ....Ballylickey House

Bray .... Glencormac House
Carrick-On-Shannon .... Bush
Dublin .... Gresham Hotel, Jury's, Moira
Galway .... Warwick
Lisdoonvarna .... Imperial, Hydro
Oughterard .... Corrib Hotel
Salthill .... Golf Links Hotel
Sutton .... Marine Hotel

FRANCE

Aix-Les-Bains .... Hotel Splendide-Royal and Excelsior, Hotel Astoria
Andorre La Vieille .... Hotel Meritxell
Annecy .... Imperial Palace, Hotel Beau-Rivage
Antibes .... Grand Hotel Du Cap d'Antibes
Avignon .... Hotel D'Europe
Bagnoles-de-L'Orne .... Lutetia-Reine Astrid
Barbotan .... Grand Hotel des Thermes
Biarritz .... Hotel Miramar, Hotel Regina Et Du Golf
Bordeaux .... Splendid-Hotel
Boulogne .... Hotel Marmin
Cannes .... Hotel Carlton, Hotel Gray d'Albion, Hotel Splendid
Chamonix .... Savoy Hotel
Deauville .... Royal, Normandy
Dijon .... Do la Cloche
Fontainebleau .... Aigle Noir
Juan-Les-Pins .... Hotel Provencal
Lourdes .... Grand Hotel De La Grotte
Lyon .... Carlton Hotel
Marseille .... Hotel Beauvau, Select Hotel
Monte Carlo .... Hotel de Paris, New Beach Hotel
Nancy .... Grand Hotel
Nantes .... Duchesse Anne
Nice .... Hotel Negresco, Hotel Royal, Hotel Westminster
Paris .... Hotel Continental, Hotel George-V, Hotel Meurice, Hotel California, Hotel Elysee-Park, Hotel Vendome
Reims .... Lion D'or
St. Jean Cap Ferrat .... Grand Hotel Du Cap Ferrat
St. Raphael .... Hotel Continental
Soissons .... Hotel Du Lion Rouge
Strasbourg .... Hotel Terminus Gruber
Touquet .... Westminster Hotel
Versailles .... Hotel Trianon-Palace
Vichy .... Thermal Palace, Elysee Palace Hotel

GERMANY

Aachen .... Kurhotel Quellenhof
Augsburg .... Parkhotel Wiesses Lamm
Baden-Baden .... Hotel Bellevue
Bad Durkheim .... Kurparkhotel
Bad Harzburg .... Bodes Hotel, Harzburger Hof
Badenweiler .... Hotel Roseneck-Kurhotel Saupe
Berlin .... Hilton, Hotel Kempinski, Hotel Fruling am Zoo, Hotel Savigny
Bonn .... Sternhotel
Bremen .... Park Hotel

Dusseldorf .... Hotel Eden
Elten-Gelderland .... Kurhotel
Frankfurt .... Hotel Frankfurter Hof, Hotel Momopol-Metropole
Garmisch .... Hotel Garmischer Hof
Hamburg .... Hotel Berlin, Hotel Continental
Heidelberg .... Schloss-Hotel
Koblenz .... Rheinhotel Koblenzerhof
Mainz/Rhein .... Hotel Mainzer Hof, Europahotel
Munich .... Bayerischer Hof, Hotel Schottenhamel
Oberammergau .... Hotel Alois Lang
Reclinghausen .... Europahotel
Tubingen .... Touring-Motel

ENGLAND
GREAT BRITAIN

Arundel .... Norfolk Arms Hotel
Ascot .... Berystede Hotel
Bath .... Pratt's Hotel
Birmingham .... Grand
Blackpool .... Imperial Hotel
Bournemouth .... Carlton, Highcliff Hotel
Brighton .... Bedford Hotel, Royal Albion
Bristol .... Grand Hotel
Burford .... The Lamb Inn
Cambridge .... Blue Boar
Canterbury .... Abbots Barton Hotel
Chester .... The Blossoms Hotel
Chipping Campden .... Noel Arms Hotel
Cirencester .... King's Head Hotel
Coventry .... The Hall Hotel
Deal .... Queen's Hotel
Doncaster .... Punch's Hotel
Dover .... White Cliffs
Droitwich Spa .... Worcestershire Hotel
East Grinstead .... Ye Olde Felbridge Hotel
Evesham .... Crown Hotel
Exeter .... Gipsy Hill Hotel
Hampton Court .... Mitre
Haslemere .... Georgian
Haytor .... Moorland Hotel
Leamington Spa .... Regent Hotel
Liverpool .... Lord Nelson
London Airport .... Skyway
London .... The Carlton Tower, Dorchester Hotel, Ritz Hotel, Savoy, Westbury, Hyde Park, Londoner, Piccadilly, Washington, Rembrandt, Rubens, St. Ermins, Green Park, Mostyn
Maidenhead .... Skindles Hotel
Manchester .... Queen's Hotel
Newcastle Upon Tyne .... Royal Turk's Head
Newmarket .... Bedford Lodge Hotel
Newquay .... Headland
Nottingham .... County Hotel
Oxford .... Mitre Hote

Plymouth .... Grand Hotel
Salisbury .... White Hart Hotel
Scarborough .... Royal Hotel
Sheffield .... Grand
Southampton .... Dolphin
Stratford-Upon-Avon .... Shakespeare
Torquay .... Imperial, Torbay, Rosetor Hotel
Weymouth .... Gloucester Hotel
Windermer .... Old England Hotel
York .... Abbey Park Hotel

SCOTLAND

Aberdeen .... Caledonian Hotel
Aviemore .... Lynwilg Hotel
Ayr .... Hotel Dalblair
Banff .... Fife Arms Hotel
Edinburgh .... Carlton, Grosvenor Hotel
Glasgow .... More's Hotel, Ivanhoe
Killin .... Killin
Pitlochry .... Fishers Hotel
St. Andrew's .... Rusack's Hotel

GREECE

Athens .... Hotel St. George, New Angleterre, Cosmopolite, Palladion
Chalkis .... Lucy Hotel
Kifissia .... Hotel Cecil, Theoxenia
Rhodes .... Hotel Des Roses
Thessaloniki .... Mediterranean Hotel

HOLLAND

Amsterdam .... Amstel Hotel, Grand Hotel Krasnapolsky
Arnheim .... Hotel Haarhuis
Delft .... Hotel Wilhelmina
Groningen .... Hotel De Doelen
Haarlem .... Hotel Lion d'Or
The Hague .... Hotel Des Indes, De Hertenkamp, Du Passage
Rotterdam .... Hotel Atlanta, Parkhotel
Utrecht .... Hotel Terminus
Zandvoort .... Hotel Bouwes

ITALY

Abano Terme .... Grand Hotel Trieste
Alassio .... Mediterranee
Cortina D'Ampezzo .... Cristallo Palace
Cremona .... Hotel Impero
Florence .... Hotel Excelsior Italie, Savoy, Grand Hotel
Gardone Riviera .... Savoy Palace
Genoa .... Colombia Excelsior Hotel
Loreto .... Grand Hotel Marchigiano
Mantova .... Jolly Hotel
Milan .... Cavalieri Hotel, Grand Hotel Continental, Garden Hotel, Diana Majestic, Palace Hotel, Principe and Savoia
Montecatini Terme .... Grand Hotel Croce di Malta
Naples .... Hotel Excelsior
Pisa .... Hotel Dei Cavalieri
Portofino .... Hotel Splendido

Rimini .... Grand Hotel
Rome .... Hotel Excelsior, Le Grand Hotel, Hassler-Villa Medici, Commodore, Bricktop's
San Remo .... Grand Hotel and Des Anglais
Sestriere .... Principi Di Piemente Hotel
Stresa .... Grand Hotel et des Iles Borromees, Regina Palace
Taormina .... S. Domenico and Grand Hotel
Torino .... Turin Palace
Venice .... Danieli Royal Excelsior, Grand Hotel Europa and Britannia, Hotel Regina and Di Roma, Excelsior Palace, Grand Hotel Des Bains and Palazzo Al Mare, Grand Hotel Lido

NORWAY

Bergen .... Orion Hotel
Fevik .... Strand Hotel
Kristiansand .... Ernst Hotel
Oslo .... Grand Hotel, Hotel Bristol
Solfonn .... Solfonn
Voss .... Fleischers Hotel

PORTUGAL

Bucaco .... Palace Hotel
Lisbon .... Ritz Hotel, Hotel Condestavel, Avenida Palace Hotel
Nazare .... Pensao Central
Porto .... Hotel Infante De Sagres, Grande Hotel Do Porto, Batalha

MEXICAN GOVT. TOURIST BD.

SPAIN

Alicante .... Hotel Carlton
Andorre La Vielle .... Hotel Meritxell
Barcelona .... Hotel Avenida Palace, Gran Hotel Cristina
Bilbao .... Hotel Carlton
Cadaques .... Rocamar Hotel
Cordoba .... Cordoba Palace
Granada .... Nevada Palace Hotel, Hotel Alhambra Palace
Lloret de Mar .... Gran Hotel Monterrey
Madrid .... Castellana Hilton, Hotel Fenix, Hotel Menfis
Playa De Aro .... Park Hotel San Jorge
Puerto De La Cruz .... Europahotel "Oro Negro"
S'Agaro .... Hostel De La Gavina

San Sebastian .... Londres E. Inglaterra
Sevilla .... Hotel Cristina, Alfonso XIII

SWEDEN

Goteborg .... Park Avenue Hotel
Granna .... Hotel Gyllene Uttern
Jonkoping .... Stora Hotellet
Malmo .... Savoy Hotel
Stockholm .... Carlton Hotel, Hotel Malmen
Tallberg .... Greens Hotell

SWITZERLAND

Aarau .... Hotel Aarauerhof
Adelboden .... Nevada Palace

UNITED NATIONS

Arosa .... Hotel Arosa-Kulm
Basel .... Hotel Trois Rois au Rhin, Hotel Greub
Gstaad .... Royal Winter and Gstaad Palace
Interlaken .... Grand Hotel Victoria-Jungfrau, Hotel Du Nord
Lausanne .... Lausanne Palace, Central Bellevue
Lucerne .... Hotel Astoria
Lugano .... Hotel Splendide-Royal, Hotel Bellevue Au Lac
Montreux .... Montreuv-Palace Hotel, Continental
St. Moritz .... Hotel Carlton, Albana
Vevey-La Tour De Peilz .... Hotel Rive-Reine
Wengen .... Palace
Zurich .... Hotel Baur Au Lac, Hotel Carlton Elite
Chateau D'Oex .... Grand Hotel du Parc
Geneva .... Hotel Beau-Rivage, de la Paix
Grindelwald .... Belvedere

AFRICA

ALGERIA

ALGIERS
Aletti .... $7 up
Albert .... $6 up
Oasis .... $5 up
Suisse .... $6 up
St. George .... $7 up

BONE
Hotel Orient .... $6 up

CONSTANTINE
Transatlantique .... $6 up

ORAN
Grand Hotel .... $7 up
Martinez .... $7 up

BURUNDI

USUMBURA
Urundi Palace........
Paguidas........
LeGrillon........

CAMEROUN

DOUALA
Akwa Palace .... $6 up
Des Cocotiers .... $8 up

GAROUA
Relais Aeriens $3.25
Relais St. Hubert $4

N'GAOUNDERE
Hauts Plateaux $3.50

Y AOUNDE
Relais Aeriens $7
Bellevue $5
Terminus $6

CENTRAL AFRICAN REPUBLIC

BANGUI
Rock Hotel .... $11 to $13

CHAD

ABECE

MOREAU

FT. LAMY
Air Hotel .... $ 9 up
du Chari .... $12 up

FT. ARCHAMBAULT
L'Escale .... $4.50 up
des Chasses .... $4.00 up
Grand Hotel .... $10 up
du Parc .... $10 up

CONGO REPUBLIC

BRAZZAVILLE

Congo Ocean .... $4 up
de Maya Maya .... $8 up
Grand .... $5 up
Relais Aeriens .... $8 up

POINTE NOIRE

Victory Palace $6
du Mayombe .... $5 up

CONGO

LEOPOLDVILLE

Astoria .... $4.50 up
Palace .... $7 up
Regina $8

BUKAVU

Riviera $7
Royal Residence .... $5 up

DAHOMEY

COTONOU

Babo .... $3 up
de la Plage .... $8 up

ETHIOPIA

ADDIS ABABA

D'Itegue .... $5 up
Ghion .... $8 up
Guenet .... $4 up
Ras .... $6 up

ASMARA

Alb. Mamasien .... $2.50 up
C.I.A.A.O. .... $6 up

GABON

LIBREVILLE

de La Residence .... $5.50 up
de l'Estuaire .... $4 up
du Roi Denis .... $8 up

LAMBARENE

de L'Ogooue .... $6 up

PT. GENTIL

du Grand Tarpon $8

GHANA

ACCRA

Ambassador .... $12 up
Lisbon .... $ 6 up
Avenida .... $10 up
Ringway .... $ 8 up

TAKORADI

Hillcrest .... $6 up
Windsor .... $6 up

GUINEA

CONAKRY

Camayenne Plage .... de France, de La Gare, du Niger

IVORY COAST

ABIDJAN

de La Vigie $3.50
du Parc .... $8 up
International .... $4 up
Le Grand .... $7 up
Relais de Cocody .... $10 up

LIBERIA

MONROVIA

Ducor Palace .... $11 up
Johnson's .... $ 8
Pan Am Hotel .... $6 to $10
Paramount .... $ 8

LIBYA

BENGHAZI

Berenice $7
Grand .... $3 up

TRIPOLI

Casino Uaddan $6
Del Mehari .... $3 up
Grand .... $3 up

MALAGASY

TANANARIVE

- Fumaroli, Terminus .... $2 up
- Lido .... $2,75 up
- Colbert $2.50
- de Franco $3.25

MALI

BAMAKO

- de La Gare .... $ 5
- Grand .... $10 up
- Le Lido .... $ 7 up
- Majestic .... $ 7 up

MAURITANIA

NOUAKCHOTT

- Oasis .... $3 up

PT. ETIENNE

- de l'Etoile .... $5 up

MOROCCO

CASABLANCA

- El Mansour .... $7 up
- Anfa .... $4 up

RABAT

- Balima .... $6 up
- Rex .... $5 up
- Tour Hassan $4

NIGER

NIAMEY

- Grand .... $8 up
- Relais Aeriens .... $5 up
- Rivoli ....
- Terminus .... $3 up

NIGERIA

LAGOS

- Ambassador .... $6 up
- Federal Palace .... $17 up

KANO

- Central .... $12 up

RWANDA

KISENYI

- Beau Sejour .... $5 up
- Bugoyi Guest House .... $8 up
- Palm Beach .... $6 up

SENEGAL

DAKAR

- Grand de N'Gor .... $8 up
- Clarice .... $5 up
- De la Croix du Sud .... $8 up
- Vichy .... $5 up
- Majestic .... $ 6

SIERRA LEONE

FREETOWN

- City Hotel .... $6 up
- Government Rest House .... $7 up
- Paramount .... $9 up
- Riviera .... $7 up

BO

- Demby .... $5 up

MAGBURAKA

- Adams .... $5 up

SOMALIA

MOGADISCIO

- Croce del Sud .... $3 up
- Giuba .... $3.50 up
- Savoia .... $2.50 up
- Scepelle .... $4 up

SUDAN

KHARTOUM

- Acropole .... $9 up
- Grand .... $7 up

TANGANYIKA

ARUSHA

New Arusha .... $6 up
Safari House .... $5.50 up

DAR ES-SALAAM

New Africa .... $6 up
Etiennes .... $4 up
Rex .... $5.50 up
Seaview .... $6 up

TANGA

Park .... $5.50 up

TOGO

LOME

Benin .... $10 up
du Golfe .... $4 up

TUNISIA

TUNIS

Majestic .... $6 up
Palace .... $7 up

UGANDA

ENTEBBE

Victoria .... $7 up

KAMPALA

Kampala Imperial .... $9 up
Speke .... $6 up

JINJA

Ripon Falls $5

MBALE

Mt. Elgon .... $7 up

UNITED ARAB REPUBLIC

CAIRO

Nile-Hilton .... $16.80 up
Longchamps .... $ 4.50 up
Continental Savoy .... $4.50 up
Semaris .... $6 up

UPPER VOLTA

OUAGADOUGOU

Central .... $8 up
de La Gare .... $4 up
Chez Fanny .... $2.50 up

BOBO-DIOULASSO

Potiniere .... $4 up
Provencal .... $3 up
Royan .... $8 up

VISA INFORMATION

Usually the traveler must have innoculation certificates for Small Pox.. Visa requirements of U. S. citizens is usually that they have a valid United States Passport and Inoculation certificates attesting to their vaccinations for Small Pox and Yellow Fever. The number of copies of the applications and photos for the applications as well as the amount of the visa fees depends on the individual countries.

GUIDE POSTS FOR A PLEASANT TRIP

By Thomasina Norford

So you're off on that "dream trip"? How can you make it really a dream trip? Or will it be a nightmare?

In travelling, like most other situations — a lot will depend on you. Knowing what to do and how to do it the easy way can mean the difference between coming home with the memories of a lifetime or saying, "Gee, I'm glad to be home".

So you have packed light and are off by car, boat, train or plane — now what?

Knowing where to stop and what is expect is provided in The Travelers Green

Book. You already know whether the place you're going to stop at, in what town, has a swimming pool or not and what other facilities are available. You have already checked on the price scale. Your reservations have been accepted and you arrive.

The first person to greet you will be the taxi driver, if you don't drive. Before you get in the taxi tell him where you are going and ask him approximately how much it will cost to get there. If the price seems exorbitant — talk to the sky cap or red cap or an official.

The next persons you meet will be the doorman and bell boy who will take your luggage into the lobby and after room assignment is made will take your luggage to the room.

Rooms vary in price. The higher up the room the more expensive, usually, and rooms "with a view" are more than inside or court rooms. Many hotels have public places such as ballrooms, rooms normally used by salesmen and party rooms. Getting on the same floor with them can be annoying. However, if you are the gregarious type — "if you can't lick 'em jine 'em."

Meals can be a joy, if you know what to order! Usually every hotel or restaurant has a house specialty. Try it. Maybe you won't like Creole Gumbo in Louisiana, but maybe you will. After all aren't you out for adventure? Then have it! If you don't like Gumbo (or any other food you've ordered) — don't blame the cook — blame only your own provincial taste and go down the street and order some ham and eggs.

So you want to "see the town"? Good! Some home work before going can be very helpful as a starter. Read some travel book, road maps and talk to some folks who have lived there. Then supplement this by a chat with some of the folks you meet in the town, such as service folk. Take a look at the picture postcards in the five and ten and take off.

If you are motoring get a road map. If you are using a sightseeing service you will know what you will see and the cost. If you are using a taxi or a private conveyance, by all means get his price and what it will cost before you engage him. It's better to hire them by the hour in most towns.

Plan your sightseeing while the townspeople are at work so as not to get involved in a traffic jam. Yes, every town has its traffic problem, or "rush hour".

So you brought the children? How nice! Well, I am sure you have prepared well for them in terms of games they can play while traveling; dressed them in comfortable clothes and told them all about the trip beforehand.

And surely you want them to have a good time, but please don't allow them to spoil other persons trips! Their "manners will be magic". Of course Papa orders all foods in the dining room. Children should come in and sit down and "act like little ladies and gentlemen" like you have trained them. This goes for public conveyances, too. And please, no running up and down the corridors and lobbies of the hotel you are in!

If you are going to visit relatives or friends in a town with the hotel as a "base of operation" call them first and find out when you will see them and for what type of activity so you will know how to dress. Then plan your other activities after that schedule is set.

So you're now ready to move to the next town or home but you must get some "gifts for the folks back home." What will it be?" Two rules are pretty simple to start with. 1. What would the recipient like? 2. What is typical of the place you've visited that fits what the person would like.

Some of the unusual things are cook books of favorite recipes of the town; charms of the most famous place or historical place: maps of the place on a hanky, scarf or towel; a travel book about the place or something that is made in the town.

Be pleasant, ask questions, don't complain (just don't go THERE again is the way to handle that!) because what you complain about will not be rectified while you are there anyway in most instances; be adventuresome; and most of all don't expect any place to be "like home". After all, that's why you took the trip in the first place, wasn't it?

THE BASEBALL CIRCUIT

AMERICAN LEAGUE

BALTIMORE ORIOLES
Memorial Stadium:
Seating capacity—49,373
33rd Street, Ellerslie Avenue,
36th Street and Ednor Rd.

CHICAGO WHITE SOX
Comiskey Park:
Seating capacity—46,550
35th Street and Shields Avenue,
Chicago 16, Ill.

CLEVELAND INDIANS
Municipal Stadium:
Seating capacity—73,811
Foot of West Third Street,
Cleveland 14, Ohio

BOSTON RED SOX
Fenway Park:
Seating capacity—33,357
Jersey Street, Landsdowne Street
and Ipswich Streets

DETROIT TIGERS
Tiger Stadium:
Seating capacity—52,850
Michigan Avenue, National Avenue,
Cherry Street and Trumbull Avenue

KANSAS CITY ATHLETICS
Municipal Stadium:
Seating capacity—32,561
Twenty-second Street and
Brooklyn Avenue

LOS ANGELES ANGELS
Chavez Stadium (Dodger Stadium):
Seating Capacity—56,000
1000 Elysian Park Avenue,
Los Angeles, Calif.

MINNESOTA TWINS
Metrpolitan Stadium:
Seating capacity—39,525
8001 Cedar Avenue,
Bloomington 20, Minn.

NEW YORK YANKEES
Yankee Stadium:
Seating capacity—70,000
East 161st Street and River Avenue,
Bronx, N. Y.

WASHINGTON SENATORS
District of Cloumbia Stadium:
Seating capacity—42,000
Twenty-second and East Capitol St.
Washington 3, D. C.

NATIONAL LEAGUE

CHICAGO CUBS
Wrigley Field
Seating capacity—36,755
Addison Street, Clark Street,
Waveland and Sheffield Avenues

HOUSTON COLT .45s
Colt Stadium:
Seating capacity—32,000
Old Spanish Trail and Main Street,
Houston, Texas

LOS ANGELES DODGERS
Dodger Stadium:
Seating capacity—56,000
1000 Elysian Park Avenue,
Los Angeles, Calif.

MILWAUKEE BRAVES
Milwaukee County Stadium:
Seating capacity—43,826
South 44th Street off Bluemound Rd.
Milwaukee 46, Wis.

NEW YORK METS
Polo Grounds:
Seating capacity—55,000
155th Street and 8th Avenue,
New York 39, N. Y.
(Shea Stadium, 126th Street and
Roosevelt Avenue, Flushing 68, N. Y.

PHILADELPHIA PHILLIES
Connie Mack Stadium:
Seating capacity—33,608
Lehigh Avenue, Somerset Street.
North 20th and North 21st Sts.
Philadelphia 32, Pa.

PITTSBURGH PIRATES
Forbes Field.
Seating capacity—35,000
Cor. of Bouquet and Sennott Streets
Pittsburgh, Pa.

ST. LOUIS CARDINALS
Busch Stadium:
Seating capacity—30,500
Grand Boulevard, Dodier Street,
Sullivan Avenue and Spring Avenues
St. Louis 7, Mo.

SAN FRANCISCO GIANTS
Candlestick Park:
Seating capacity—42,500
Bayshore Blvd., San Francisco, Caif.

CURRENCY EXCHANGE

The following list gives the approximate rates of exchange, quoted on the U.S.A. dollar, as we went to press. Since exchange rates vary from day to day, to be accurate it is advisable that you check with your bank or travel agent.

CURRENCY EXCHANGE		per U.S.$
AUSTRIA	Shilling (Groschen)	26
BELGIUM	Franc (Centimes)	50
DENMARK	Kroner	6.90
FRANCE	Nouveau Franc	4.90
GERMANY	Deutschmark (pfennig)	4.001
GREAT BRITAIN	Pounds (Shillings and Pennies)	7/-
GREECE	Drachma	30
HOLLAND	Gulder (Cent)	3.60
ITALY	Lire	620
NORWAY	Kroner (Ore)	7.1
PORTUGAL	Escudo (Centavo)	28.50
SPAIN	Peseta (Centimo)	59
SWEDEN	Kroner (Ore)	5.17
SWITZERLAND	Franc (Centimes)	4.31
YUGOSLAVIA	Dinar	700
CANADA		1.08
BRAZIL	Free Fluctuating	
COLOMBIA	Free Fluctuating	
EGYPT	(Pound-100 piastres)	.434
MEXICO	Peso	.08

green book's

HISTORY-MAKERS

William A. LEIDESDORFF

IN 1847, THREE YEARS AFTER THIS SEAMAN FROM THE VIRGIN ISLANDS BECAME A NATURALIZED CITIZEN, HE LAUNCHED THE FIRST STEAMBOAT IN SAN FRANCISCO BAY! A SUCCESSFUL BUSINESSMAN, HE BUILT FRISCO'S 1ST HOTEL, WAS A MEMBER OF THE 1ST TOWN COUNCIL & SCHOOL BOARD & WAS CITY TREASURER! LEIDESDORFF ALSO ORGANIZED THE 1ST HORSE-RACING IN CALIFORNIA AND HAS STREET NAMED FOR HIM.

TRAVELING TRUNKLINES

Have most of your travel wardrobe wash 'n' wear. A dip, splash and drip keeps your things fresh as a daisy.

Simple, basic travel togs save space. As usual, hubby won't need much . . . slacks, several jackets, etc. will keep him neat. You can give the impression of a large wardrobe with an interesting variety of accessories without excess luggage.

Pack heavier articles together at the bottom of the suitcase and the larger garments, carefully and smoothly folded, over them. Keep plastic bags that those new shirts came in for shoes. Put toiletries in leakproof containers. This will save your things from damage. By-the-way, the things you use first or most often put them on top.

Be protected. Go to the bank and get travelers' checks. These are replaceable and always negotiable.

Don't forget the weather, girls! Unless you're going au naturel, have enough 'hair aids' to keep you confident in humid or dry conditions.

DEAR READERS:

During 27 dedicated years of publishing your Travelers' GREEN BOOK we have constantly sought to improve our service to you. We want you to enjoy yourself. In fact, we are in business to help you "VACATION WITHOUT AGGRAVATION."

If you will drop us a line and tell us how you enjoyed your travel accommodations, we certainly would appreciate it. If you have any suggestions how we can be of more help, let us know . . . it will help us to maintain our high standards and keep Travelers' GREEN BOOK your favorite travel guide.

Sincerely,
Victor H. Green Co.

History

The Negro Motorist Green Book, first published in 1936, was a product of the rising African-American middle class having the finances and vehicles for travel but facing a world where social and legal restrictions barred them from many accomodations. At the time, there were thousands of "sundown towns", places where African Americans were legally barred from spending the night there at all.

Victor H. Green
1892 – 1960

The book provided a guide to hotels and restaurants that would accept their business, often ones established specifically for the black customer. Published annually by Victor Hugo Green, a New Yorker who retired from his work as a mailman based on its success and expanded into the travel reservation business, the *Green Book* was for decades a vital handbook, fading out of business only after the civil rights laws of the 1960s brought about the end of legal segregation. It was sold largely through mail order and through service stations - specifically, through Esso stations, as Esso not only served African-American customers, they were willing to franchise their stations to African-Americans, unlike most petroleum companies of the day. The guide was also offered by AAA and distributed elsewhere with advice from the United States Travel Bureau, a government agency.

Green passed away in 1960, not quite living to see the legal changes in 1964 that would eliminate much of the need for his guide. The Green Book continued in other hands for several years.

Facsimile edition published by About Comics, Camarillo, California. The publisher thanks the Schomburg Center for Research in Black Culture for access that made this edition possible. Address inquries to questions@aboutcomics.com. *First printing: April, 2017. This printing: May, 2019.*